HERE'S WHAT PEOPLE ARE SAYING ABOUT SHELLIE TOMLINSON AND *DON'T TRY TO PRAY LIKE HER*...

As a detective, I've spent my career searching for the kinds of practical, evidence-based advice that help people thrive in their daily life and faith. *Don't Try to Pray Like Her* might sound like a book written with women in mind but make no mistake about it, Shellie Tomlinson has packed these pages with wisdom that men will find just as transformational. Shellie's candid stories and practical habits will help you draw near to Jesus with confidence, not by imitating others, but by discovering what authentic prayer is like in your own walk with God. Whether you're a husband, father, or just looking for a deeper relationship with God, this book is filled with the kind of evidence-based encouragement I depend on in my own faith journey.

—J. Warner Wallace
Senior fellow, Colson Center for Christian Worldview
Author, *Cold-Case Christianity*

Like the author, I once gazed at prayer champion church ladies, thinking, "That will never be me." What changed? I can't say, but Shellie can! She tracked her meander from "Whoa, those prayer ladies are awesome aliens" to fifteen ways to finding your way in prayer.

—Dr. Naomi Cramer Overton, MBA
Founder and CEO, Becoming
Host, *Every Woman's Story* podcast

This book will make you laugh and smile, but most of all, it will make you want to pray. Shellie Tomlinson writes like a friend. You can feel her hugs as you read, and you will be drawn into having a more meaningful conversation with God with every chapter.

—Arlene Pellicane
Author, *Grandparenting Screen Kids*
Host, *Happy Home* podcast

Shellie has a deep, warm relationship with God that oozes through her writing. If you are looking for a guide to help you approach God in a way that is true to how He created you, this book is for you!

—*Laurie Short*
Author, *40 Verses to Ignite Your Faith*

If you're longing to learn how to more intimately connect with God through prayer, then this resource is for you! Shellie Tomlinson is a fellow sojourner who is steps ahead of you in learning to enjoy God's presence through heartfelt intercession. Walking through these pages with Shellie feels like I'm having a wonderful conversation with a beloved friend who's been in my shoes. The engaging stories and practical applications are bathed in biblical truths with the potential to transform the way you draw near to God in prayer. In each chapter, I found many inspiring nuggets to ponder and apply. I was especially uplifted by this, my favorite quote: "Real words equal humility, and humble humans encounter God."

—*Rhonda Stoppe*
Host, *Old Ladies Know Stuff* podcast
Author, *Moms Raising Sons to Be Men*

If you've ever panicked when asked to pray out loud, grown restless when someone prayed too long, wondered why your own prayers seemed to bounce off the ceiling, or marveled at the eloquence of someone else's prayers—this book is for you. Shellie shares fifteen honest stories with practical takeaways. Guaranteed, at least three or four will speak directly to your own prayer life.

—*Jay Payleitner*
Best-selling author, *52 Things Kids Need from a Dad*

You know God is answering prayer when this book arrives in your in-box the same day you asked Jesus to help you pray better. Shellie has captured the angst of the heart's desire to pray while giving us permission to do it in the unique way in which God made us. This is a freeing book on prayer while being told in the storytelling, Jesus-loving, and heart-connecting way that Shellie knows how to do so beautifully.

—*Denise Jones*
Author, *Reclaiming Your Heart*

DON'T TRY TO PRAY LIKE HER

Fifteen Simple Habits to Enjoy a Realer, Richer Prayer Life

SHELLIE RUSHING
TOMLINSON

WHITAKER
HOUSE

Don't Try to Pray Like Her

Fifteen Simple Habits to Enjoy a Realer, Richer Prayer Life

shelliet.com
www.facebook.com/Shellierushingtomlinson

ISBN: 979-8-88769-598-3 | eBook ISBN: 979-8-88769-599-0
Printed in the United States of America

Whitaker House | 1030 Hunt Valley Circle | New Kensington, PA 15068
www.whitakerhouse.com

Library of Congress Cataloging-in-Publication Data
Names: Tomlinson, Shellie Rushing author
Title: Don't try to pray like her : fifteen simple habits to enjoy a realer, richer prayer life / Shellie Rushing Tomlinson.
Description: New Kensington, PA : Whitaker House, 2025. | Summary: "With Scripture passages and humorous personal stories, offers fifteen practical prayer habits that believers can use to learn how to pray their own way and develop confidence that God wants to hear from them no matter what"— Provided by publisher.
Identifiers: LCCN 2025032516 (print) | LCCN 2025032517 (ebook) | ISBN 9798887695983 trade paperback | ISBN 9798887695990 ebook
Subjects: LCSH: Prayer—Christianity
Classification: LCC BV215 .T575 2025 (print) | LCC BV215 (ebook)
LC record available at https://lccn.loc.gov/2025032516
LC ebook record available at https://lccn.loc.gov/2025032517

1 2 3 4 5 6 7 8 9 10 11 ꟺ 33 32 31 30 29 28 27 26

DEDICATION

To anyone who has ever wanted a prayer life that seemed impossibly out of reach, you are not alone. Come with me and let us go to God.

—Hugs, Shellie

And the Spirit and the bride say, "Come!"

—Revelation 22:17 (NKJV)

CONTENTS

FOREWORD

When I was a child, I watched my dad on many occasions furrow his brow, look to the sky, and speak softly, so softly that I could never hear exactly what he was saying. This happened multiple times a day and in every place we would be—in the car, at the dinner table, even during my sporting events in front of my friends! Oh, the horror! What was he doing? It even happened in the middle of my conversations with him.

One day I asked my dad, "Who are you talking to and why are you not paying attention to what I'm saying?" He abruptly turned to me and answered, "Oh, I'm sorry, Baby, I didn't mean to be rude. I was talking to the Father." I realized then, at a very early age, that my dad took everything in his thoughts and in his conversations, even in the middle of them, directly to the Father, no matter what was happening around him. He talked to Him all day long. I even learned to recognize his *prayer face* and would wait until he was finished before I started talking to my dad. I knew my dad's relationship with God was the most important thing, and I learned to respect that.

Through that, I learned that God wants to hear what we're feeling, thinking, and hoping as soon as we're feeling them, thinking about them, and hoping for them. He also wants to hear our anguished cries for things to change in our lives. This was not always possible, you know. The Father was not always accessible to His children except through rituals and sacrifices and then only through one priest who would carry the full burden of all the people directly into the holy of holies and only once a year! But once Jesus—the perfect Lamb, the ultimate sacrifice, and the fulfillment of the Law and all rituals—was sacrificed for our iniquities, that curtain was ripped from top to bottom and the holy of holies was then exposed and accessible for us to walk directly into the arms of our Father, sit on His lap, and tell Him everything happening in our lives. And even when we can't get the words out, the Spirit living inside of us makes it all make sense to our Father.

Shellie breaks this type of real-time prayer down to fifteen simple practices to help us focus on living a daily conversation with our God. It may seem overwhelming at first. When she told me the subtitle, I thought, "There are fifteen ways? Yikes!" However, if you have a relationship with your Savior, you will quickly become aware of just how many of these practices you are already accomplishing each day and maybe be open to some challenges to add a couple more to your intentional walk with God.

If you do not have that relationship, Shellie gives you easy ways to start. God is waiting on each one of us. He's seeking us. He wants a relationship with us. When I remember this, I want to be in His arms more and more. They're open and waiting for me and for you. Step into them and settle in, lay your head on His chest and feel His warmth, His strength, His comfort, His joy for you, His compassion, His goodness, His love. Everything He has done for us flows directly from His love for us. Once you get to know Him, you'll find yourself longing to share your life with Him. Step into the holy of holies.

BlesSINGs,
Missy Robertson

INTRODUCTION

There was a time when prayer was absolutely hands down, without a doubt, the last topic I could have imagined myself writing and speaking on ... and yet, here I am. I can tell you I love prayer now and feel God witness to that statement, but He and I remember when a healthy prayer life felt impossibly out of reach to me, despite my longing for it. One of the reasons I was mired in prayer shame is because I was always operating under what my friend Curtis Wilson calls "the pass/fail mentality." I acted like God was overseeing my prayer progress and giving me a passing or failing grade. Only, good parents don't raise their kids in a pass/fail system, and our God is the ultimate good Father. He doesn't give us one shot to get it right and give up on us when we miss the mark. No, God nurtures His children, raising us up to know Him more intimately and love Him all the more.

These days, I assure you through personal experience that Holy Spirit is a faithful Teacher to all who want to be taught! My testimony is that He is ever teaching. Even now, as I set out to write on prayer, I am nothing more than a wide-eyed pupil taking in the wonder of His invite. He is Instructor, holding my hand and leading me deeper into prayer's marvels and mysteries. I am a preschooler walking into the first day of class, filled with nervous excitement about what's ahead, knowing there's more I don't know than what I do know. Indeed, after a long season searching for the secrets to prayer that always seemed so elusive, I find the big door to God's presence has finally swung open for me and I dearly love it here.

On the outside chance that analogy didn't clue you in, here's a heads-up. You won't find a point-by-point doctrinal breakdown on prayer in these pages, and you won't need a seminary degree to follow me. What you will get are prayer habits for the rest of us. I'm determined to write without pretense so you can find value in my words. I'm convinced it didn't have to take me anywhere near as long as it did to discover a prayer life that somehow manages to both nourish my soul and cause my faith to grow, while simultaneously humbling me and leaving me craving more. But I'll consider all my hits and misses worth the cost if my experiences can help you get to Jesus sooner and come to love Him more.

To make sure we understand each other at the onset, let me clarify what I mean when I say I once longed for a healthy prayer life. I'm not talking about reading written prayers, bringing a list of requests to God, or even praying the Scriptures. I do all these things; I believe there's a time and place for each of them, and we'll touch on all of them in these pages. But my experience has been that those good practices do little to satisfy my heart's desire for intimacy with God. Reading a prayer or offering a petition doesn't humble and challenge me either, at least not in the way wanting to learn how to sit with God and be with Him consistently exposes my neediness. And, boy, does it ever! My desire to experience God in prayer regularly strips me of all confidence in me. Could this be by holy design? I think so.

I remember pouring my heart out once to a fellow believer who has my utmost respect, someone I know to be devoted to prayer. My earnest confession was born of utter frustration and my complaints sounded like this: "I can read Scripture prayers, and I can make prayer requests, but for the life of me, I can't figure out how to be with God and listen for Him without me doing all the talking! Every time I try to sit quietly, my mind wanders, so I feel like I have to start praying again. I don't know how I'm ever going to hear Him over me! And that's not all. When I try to pray with my eyes open, I get distracted by everything around me, but if I close my eyes to pray, I have to fight drowsiness and try not to fall asleep!"

I'm sure I said a lot more than that, but that's the gist of my rant. I was humbled, confused, and hurting. I was Peter confessing to Jesus that I didn't want to leave Him because I was convinced that He alone held the words of life, but I didn't understand where we were going or how we were meant to get there! (See John 6:60–71.) My heart was sore and desperate for answers. If prayer was what God wanted, and a prayer life was what I wanted, why was praying so hard? Does any of that sound familiar? Are you waiting for the big secret? I was too. I didn't get one.

I can remember so much of that conversation, including where we were sitting and the understanding look in the other person's eyes. What I don't remember is getting any game-changing, or better still, prayer-changing advice. Was sound counsel offered that day that went right over my head? Did it fall on ears that weren't ready to hear? Or was the help I was crying out for not given? Your guess is as good as mine. I remain as deeply inspired by this saint as I was when this incident happened, so if there is any blame to be placed, I place it squarely on my hearing ears. The bottom line: I didn't get an answer. There would be no shortcut for me, no map to lead me out of the maze of me—and maybe, just maybe, that was providential. Spiritual desperation is a blessing, and God is a *"rewarder of those who diligently seek Him"* (Hebrews 11:6 NKJV).

I share that story for anyone who has ever felt like a life of prayer is unattainable. Have you ever wondered how some people learn to be with God, how they talk of *hearing* God, when you can't seem to get anywhere in prayer? You're not alone. You have more human company than you could ever number. But here's some glorious news: You also sit in the company of your God, and He wants you to know Him more than you want to know Him! He so desired this restored relationship that He left His throne in heaven and took on flesh to make it happen. The path back to God, long barred by angels and *"a flaming sword"* (Genesis 3:24 NKJV) was reopened by Jesus His Son, who is the exact representation of His Father. Jesus died on the cross for our sins to redeem us and restore the privilege of knowing God. This is meant to be a shared joy! It's yours, it's His, and it's past time for you to begin enjoying your inheritance. I want to help.

GOD WANTS YOU TO KNOW HIM MORE THAN YOU WANT TO KNOW HIM!

There are many forms of prayer. There's confession and thanksgiving, intercession and petition, praise, supplication, meditation, and adoration. That list is far from exhaustive, and those forms overlap. They're each important and we may touch on all of them before we're done, but the prayer habits I'll be sharing fall best in the categories of meditation and adoration, the individual believer's pursuit of God's company.

My musings are for those hungry to walk with God, who long to enjoy prayer. I offer them for anyone desperate to figure out how to spend time with Him. These habits are for those who are refusing to settle for anything less than knowing Jesus more. I'm talking about a relationship Paul calls the *"fellowship of the Spirit"* (Philippians 2:1).

The Spirit's fellowship is the gift of eternal life. He is our unreplaceable, incomparable prayer partner and tutor, who guides and empowers our prayers and receives them. He is all in all. Prayer that finds God's ear is birthed by the Spirit of God in us and sustained by our surrender to His leading. And speaking frankly, we're unlikely to engage in intercession, petition, or any other form of prayer without learning how to be with God. Until we discover how to find delight and satisfaction in God's presence, we'll stayed mired in our nonexistent prayer lives and secretive about our failure. Oh, we may read our written prayers and rattle off our petitions, but our efforts will be well-meaning exercises in religion at best. They won't feed our souls. Ask me how I know.

A word about this book's title: *Don't Try to Pray Like Her* is a nod to my determination to vaccinate all of us against the disease of comparison. Regardless of how many blogs, books, Bible studies, and podcasts we've read on the dangers of comparing ourselves, we're still ridiculously susceptible to this ugly virus! Did I hear a whispered amen? I get it. Remember how I said there was a time when prayer was "absolutely hands down, without a doubt, the last topic I could have imagined myself writing" about? I'm not immune to those destructive feelings of comparison. They can still come; they just present themselves a little differently. As much as I've come to love prayer, I do life with people whose beautiful flowing prayers could lead me to second-guess whether I'm the right woman to even write this book. "Perhaps," the doubts whisper, "you should stay in safer, more familiar waters." Oh, but I said their prayers *could* make me insecure about writing on prayer. Hold on to that thought; I'm coming right back to it.

These other believers are never at a loss for words. Maybe you know them or someone like them. They seem to pray by an outline in their heads that moves from point A to point B, well-articulated subpoints included, without ever pausing or searching for what they want to say next. Their prayers are beautiful, inspiring, intimate, and yes, potentially intimidating. But here's what I know. *Comparison is kryptonite to a believer's prayer life, and God's presence is the anecdote.*

So, yes, while other believers *could* make me second-guess writing to you, thankfully, walking and talking with God is inoculating me against those doubts and fortifying my resolve. I'm an insecure scribe, confident only as far as I'm leaning on Jesus and I'm happy to own that. I've often said our greatest strength is realizing Jesus is our greatest need. I am His, and He is mine, and His otherworldly love is steady reassurance. This is the kind of experience that drives me to share what I'm learning on the journey, despite knowing I have so much more to learn! I want you to be enjoying God's company and thriving in His presence too. And when you do, don't be surprised to find you want to pass it on. It's a beauty of a plan and not one of us had a hand in its divine design. Praise Him.

In the following chapters, I'll share fifteen prayer supports or habits I've discovered in my quest to walk this earth with God. Each chapter will concentrate on a single piece of advice. It's heart-to-heart counsel meant to share easy-to-remember aids you can carry on your own prayer journey. You can go to Shelliet.com/prayeraids for a downloadable bookmark to print for easy reference. You might want to put it in your Bible or near your favorite prayer spot. These habits-speak to the questions I didn't or couldn't get answered from the seasoned saint I mentioned earlier and they've come as I've continued to lay those same pleadings before the greatest Teacher in the universe. Apart from the initial offering, which underscores our foundation in prayer, I won't be sharing my discoveries in any particular order. They aren't steps to follow or parts of a larger formula. Walking with God isn't a process that we must strive to perfect. Every time we reach for God in prayer is a fresh opportunity to know Him more, not a box we check to please Him.

The aids I'll be sharing in this project are ones I still use, and as Holy Spirit prompts, I'll be adding whatever I'm learning in real time as we travel through these pages together. It's my joy to write of both what I've learned and what I'm learning because I don't ever want to get far from this golden truth: It is the present tense ongoing ministry of Holy Spirit who teaches us to pray. He is our Helper. If we want to learn to pray, we must begin by asking Holy Spirit to teach us how, and we must never stop asking for His help.

Jesus said, *"I will ask the Father, and He will give you another Helper, so that He may be with you forever; the Helper is the Spirit of truth, whom the world cannot receive, because it does not see Him or know Him; but you know Him because He remains with you and will be in you"* (John 14:16–17). And Romans 8:26 tells us Holy Spirit not only helps us pray because we don't know how, He also guides us in praying God's will. Being a student in the Spirit's school offers real-time instruction that becomes the sweetest of addictions. Why? Because unlike human teachers who come and go in our lives, Holy Spirit remains after the lesson to help us practice it and empower us to walk it out.

For example, I'm presently thrilling to a recent revelation of something Holy Spirit has *made me to know* that is so fresh, so exhilarating, I keep reaching for its life-giving succor over and again. *Made me to know* is my best definition of how I hear God's inside voice speaking to my soul. I simply don't know something... and then I *do*. I've found these impressions from God often arrive in my heart quietly and unexpectedly, but they come with great staying power. It's a ginormous mistake to trust every thought that comes to us—that's a book in itself!—but we can learn to recognize the Lord's voice. Better still, we're meant to have this discernment. Jesus explained, *"But the Advocate, the Holy Spirit, whom the Father will send in my name, will teach you all things and will remind you of everything I have said to you"* (John 14:26 NIV).

GOD IS NOT GRADING OUR PRAYERS;
HE JUST WANTS US TO PRAY!

Without discernment, we're easy targets for the enemy's endless insistent accusations, but as we learn the language of the Spirit, our hearing becomes attuned to the voice of our Beloved. We begin to recognize the Spirit's voice as we discover that Jesus convicts without condemning, and He counsels without crushing. The result? We find ourselves running to His correction, not from it!

We'll talk more about differentiating between the different impressions that come to us as we seek to hear the Spirit's voice. For now, here's more on that recent revelation Jesus made me to know. After all this time learning and thrilling to His ways, and despite my growing enjoyment in prayer, Jesus showed me I still have a tendency to treat my times with Him as if they're acts of devotion to complete, sign, and turn in for His approval. Wow. Really, Jesus? I was surprised when that impression first began taking shape in my thoughts, and honestly, I was resistant to it. Not that I haven't done that sort of thing in the past. I have. I even wrote about the trap of performing my prayers in my book *Finding Deep and Wide* because I wanted to help others avoid it. Here are those words from your teacher who is ever being taught.

> *Dear reader, I want to offer you something I call my Forever Prayer… Father God, grant me this forever prayer, that You would always stop me when I'm trying to woo You with my praise, when I'm evaluating me as the gauge of my right to draw near to You, and when I'm trying to make a good sounding prayer instead of talking to You, and remind me that my access to You is through Jesus alone and true life is found in being aware of and yielding to You, the ever present and eternal God who is right here, right now.*[1]

So, yes, I have a lot of history with learning how to submit my Type A, *make it happen* personality to Jesus. I've recognized my *earn it* mentality surfacing in a myriad of ways and I've had to crucify all of them. But in full transparency, I thought I knew better now, and I felt like I was beyond that where it concerns prayer because I enjoy it so much these days. And yet, here was Jesus, telling me my feet were falling into the familiar trap of earning my right to enjoy Him. Really? Again?! My first response was, "Ugh!" However, the more I allow Him to remind me, yet again, that He has done it all and I get all the benefits of His finished work, the sweeter His presence becomes. As a result, instead of feeling frustrated by my remedial self, I'm thinking how kind it is of Him to answer my forever prayer!

---

1. Shellie Rushing Tomlinson, *Finding Deep and Wide: Stop Settling for the Life You Have and Live the One Jesus Died to Give You* (Washington, DC: Salem Books, 2020).

There is nothing we have done and nothing we can do to add to what Christ has done to present us approved and reconciled to God. When we come to prayer like it is something we must do well to gain His approval and enjoy His company, we're left pushing, pulling, and struggling to access a relationship that is already ours.

I'm having a wonderful time celebrating this old thought that's new again with the Lover of my soul who is speaking it to me. Morning by morning, I'm telling God how grateful I am that I don't have anything to accomplish when I approach Him. He isn't one more person for you and me to tend to or care for. He isn't needy. We are. Our privilege is to adore Him, to explore the wonder of His being, and immerse ourselves in Him today and forever, listening for His voice. We are safe to leave our agendas at His door and trust Him to put the petitions and intercessions on our hearts that are moving His. It is lingering in His presence and saturating ourselves in His Word and in prayer that transforms us day by day, giving us hearts that want to obey Him and ears that learn to hear Him. He transforms and we abide. Somehow, regardless of how many times this thought comes to me and I express my gratitude over it to God, He and I enjoy the truth again, together. It's a mystery that's higher than me and better than anything I could have ever hoped to experience.

Jesus promises us that, *"My sheep hear my voice"* (John 10:27 ESV). Learning to trust that we're hearing from Him is a process and the Spirit is willing to teach us day by day, line upon line. The Spirit speaks in many ways. He calls to us through nature, through other believers, and through our own impressions, but here's our safeguard: He will never ever contradict His written Word. If we think God is speaking, but we're not sure, we can go to His Word for that blessed assurance every time. Allow me to show you what that can look like.

I'm sure you agree saying God *made me to know* as I did earlier is strange phrasing. (It's okay to admit it. I said it first!) I had used the words more than a few times in conversation with other believers before I brought it up to God in prayer one morning. I wanted to know where that phrase came from and why it felt so right. I was literally asking Him if it was biblical when the words *inward parts* bubbled up in my spirit. Now, I don't know about you, but I don't go around using words like "inward parts" either and yet, there they were. They had dropped in my heart so quickly and they had staying power. That combination was motivation enough for me, so I did a Bible search on the words "inward parts." (Translation: I googled.)

I literally laughed out loud as I read the following words: "*Behold, You desire truth in the inward parts, and in the hidden part You will* ***make me to know*** *wisdom*" (Psalm 51:6 NKJV). Now, beyond the fact that I'm not smart enough to make up that kind of story, it underscores a truth we can't afford to miss. God was breathing on His words that are stored in my heart, even though I wasn't consciously aware of them. That, my friend, is an early advertisement for one of our prayer supports. I'm looking forward to talking to you about how we can prepare to hear God speaking to us by actively planting His Word in our hearts.

Oh, we have so much to learn together, and the Spirit of God is waiting to teach. Come with me and let's go to Him.

Hugs,
Shellie

PRAYER HABIT #1

REMEMBER TO USE THE DOOR

~HUGS, SHELLIE

1

I AM RUNNING FOR THE DOOR; RUN WITH ME

Habit #1 – Remember to use the Door.

The names and details in the following story have been changed to protect the not-so-innocent. (That would be me. The need for anonymity will be clear soon enough.)

Years ago, when Jason and Jim were still young boys, their family went on a trip to visit out-of-state relatives. The two brothers were spending the night in a guest room furnished with a set of bunk beds. Jim, the oldest, had snagged the bottom bunk, leaving Jason to climb to the top.

At some point during the night, Jason awoke with an urgent need for a bathroom. It took him a minute to remember where he was but once he got his bearings, he climbed down from the top bunk and was immediately confronted with a more pressing problem. Where was the door that opened to the hall? Jason couldn't remember and the unfamiliar room was pitch black. He began feeling his way along the walls, to no avail. Jason groped his way around the room for what felt like hours but was probably closer to seconds. Meanwhile, his wake-up call was growing in intensity.

Young Jason finally decided on a plan of action. Fair warning. You and I are going to feel like he had other options, such as waking Jim for help, but sometimes when you're under pressure (so to speak), you can't think clearly. Which is why Jason slipped into his big brother's bed and relieved himself before crawling back to the top bunk and falling asleep where it was nice and dry.

I wasn't given the full details of what happened early the next morning when a surprised and totally mortified Jim woke up in cold wet sheets. Unfortunately, neither was he. It was years before Jason came clean, and even longer before older brother quit dreaming of ways to make little brother pay. Being the youngest of three, I get that too.

A book on prayer opening with this story may surprise you, but I lead with it because I do love a good chuckle, and because it illustrates the importance of locating the door. Nothing I can say about prayer going forward will amount to a hill of beans if you and I don't understand the golden truth I aim to unpack about the door in this first chapter and, more importantly, *learn how to put it into practice.*

I emphasized that last phrase because being told what we should do is frustrating if we can't figure out how to do what's being asked of us. This is true in any area of our lives but spiritually speaking commandments alone, minus the understanding and power to keep them, will always leave us mired in shame and condemnation. Let me show you what this looks like for any believer who gets distracted right after, "Dear Lord…" and loses focus way before "amen."

We know praying is a commandment, not just a good idea. We know Jesus said, "***When** you pray*" (Matthew 6:5) and not "*if* you pray" and we know 1 Thessalonians 5:17 instructs us to, "*Pray without ceasing.*" The problem is none of those commandments to pray birth a love for prayer in any of us. You don't have to make eye contact, but you know I'm right. I'm going to take a wild guess that you don't need to hear yet another person in your life saying you should pray. It's the doing that can be our undoing.

And why? For starters, if we haven't come to enjoy prayer, our enemy will use those very commands to pray to remind us that we don't. Our foe has studied us for centuries and he knows our tendency when we're confronted with our sin is to rationalize it or bury it instead of running to Jesus with it. But then, I'm assuming you know you have a supernatural enemy, and maybe you don't, so let's establish two facts at the outset. We do have an enemy, and he is determined to keep us from developing any kind of prayer life. The Bible refers to him as Satan and 1 Peter 5:8 (ESV) calls him our adversary: *"Be sober-minded; be watchful. Your adversary the devil prowls around like a roaring lion, seeking someone to devour."*

We could deep dive here with more information about the devil but that's not the book I'm setting out to write. My sole purpose in mentioning him is because it's critical for us to understand that our desire to pray is met with fierce opposition from this foe. If you're a believer, the devil has lost the battle for your soul, but he'll never quit trying to keep you out of God's presence. Our enemy knows something we're inclined to forget. It's God's presence and God's Word that incrementally transform believers into light bearers that point others to Jesus. This is why he does all he can to keep us trapped in the ugly cycle of trying to pray, failing to pray, and hiding the evidence that we don't pray.

That was the bad news, but it's powerless once we grasp the good news! There's an open door that leads us out of the dead-end halls of that maze. This door opens into a beautiful, broad place where the presence of God waits to empower us for anything He asks of us and that includes—somebody celebrate with me!—the admonition to pray.

The apostle Paul wrote of our powerful new access to supernatural living in his famous passage in Romans chapter 7 but before celebrating the solution, he set up the problem with these words:

> *I would not have come to know sin except through the Law; for I would not have known about coveting if the Law had not said, "You shall not covet." But sin, taking an opportunity through the commandment, produced in me coveting of every kind; for apart from the Law sin is dead. I was once alive apart from the Law; but when the commandment came, sin came to life, and I died; and this commandment, which was to result in life, proved to result in death for me.*
>
> (Romans 7:7–10)

Wow. Paul just admitted it was the command not to covet that made him realize he couldn't quit coveting! This is what sin does with any and every law we try to obey. That's sobering, but there's more. Paul said this realization (that he couldn't quit coveting) became a death sentence for him. Those are strong words, but Paul doubles down on them throughout his teachings. In his letter to the Corinthian church, he writes, *"For the letter [of the Law] kills [by revealing sin and demanding obedience], but the Spirit gives life"* (2 Corinthians 3:6 AMP).

But why does the law kill, Paul? Isn't that our question? The answer is because it exposes our inability to obey God. The law reveals our preference for ourselves, our persistent fondness for our agenda, our ways, our plans, and our self-rule, or what John Calvin calls "the pestilence of our self-interest." This preference for our wants over God's will is the root of all sin, and Romans 6:23 tells us, *"The wages of sin is death."* In other words, sin produces death because sin separates us from God, who is *life*.

Perhaps you're thinking, "But wait, Shellie. I'm a believer. My old self died with Christ, and I've been made new!" I hear you, and I'm ecstatic that you're in Christ Jesus, but are you telling me you're never tempted to say or do anything that doesn't line up with God's will and you're always eager to do what God says to do as soon as you know to do it? I didn't think so. Because our spirits are indeed born again when we come to faith in Christ, but our souls, our wills, are alive and kicking. The push and pull between God's will and our own self-interests will be with us as long as we're living on this side of glory.

So back to our dilemma. Hearing we should pray when we can't seem to pray exposes the chasm between the commandment and our inability to keep it, and we're left with shame and condemnation. Death separating us from life. That sets up the problem. What you and I need is the enabling power to pray, and it is readily available. Better said, He is available! Jesus is the solution.

Let's look at Paul's jubilant conclusion, for Paul found a way out the maze of self. Paul discovered the gospel-given escape route from the vicious cycle of his good intentions defeating him and his enemy always mocking him because he couldn't see them through. Paul writes:

> *So I find it to be a law that when I want to do right, evil lies close at hand. For I delight in the law of God, in my inner being, but I see in my members another law waging war against the law of my mind and making me captive to the law of sin that dwells in my members. Wretched man that I am! Who will deliver me from this body of death? Thanks be to God through Jesus Christ our Lord!* (Romans 7:21–25 ESV)

The Word doesn't tell us what Paul looked like and sounded like when he was making this big announcement, but it's obvious his words built up to a celebration. Can you bear with a little imagery from my heart? I picture a very expressive Paul, using words and hand motions to share his startling discovery. I see him calling out to his friends. Maybe he even grabs the face of a struggling believer between his hands as he shouts, "I get it! I know the ugly cycle of trying and failing. I know it too well, but just when I was convinced there was no way out of the maze of me, I found an open door!"

The way Paul is celebrating is open for every believer. His victory can be ours! If we grasp the truth Paul is announcing, we'll be shouting too. *Jesus lives in us to empower us to do and be what God asks us to do and be!*

Christ's finished work enables us to say no to our fallen nature and yes to what God asks of us—and that includes the commandment to pray! Jesus is *"the door"* (John 10:9), the Way out of ourselves and into the life of God. But what does that look like? Better yet, how can it help you pray? I intend to explain. Celebrating Jesus as *"the door"* is one of my favorite subjects, but I'm reminding myself to show some restraint and keep my thoughts on it to a healthy minimum, or you'll be running for the hills before we get to chapter 2!

JESUS IS THE DOOR OUT OF OURSELVES AND INTO THE LIFE OF GOD.

I'm learning that prayer humbles me day in and day out because it is always bringing me face to face with the kind of naked awareness of my inability to do what I want to do, just as the law once did for an exasperated Paul. Let me be clearer still. I can experience the most fulfilling prayer time with God today and chase my thoughts in a circle when I reach for Him tomorrow. It's an overused cliché, but the struggle is real! And yet this humbling reality is simultaneously extending to me the most priceless gift imaginable *if* I allow it to remind me of my desperate need for Jesus and *if* I respond by hightailing it to *"the door."* The sin of my fallen nature and the death that is separation from the life of God lose every single time I take my sins, weaknesses, and failures in my sweaty hands and run back to the all-sufficiency of Jesus's cross.

See, regardless of the command, the answer remains the same. When we can't do what God is asking us to do, we can take our challenged, needy selves and run to the One who opened up the Way back to His Father and ours, Jesus the Son, Jesus the door. He is our forever source. He is where we find fresh supplies of all we need. In Christ Jesus, God supplies what God asks for. Praise Him. It does not matter what the commandment is, Christ's finished work is the way out of our powerlessness to obey it, every single time. I get it. I still need to explain how this truth helps us pray. Stay with me while I connect more dots.

Someone once said prayer is "like quietly opening a door and slipping into the very presence of God." I love that quote. I'm not trying to improve on it, but it is to our great advantage to live reminding ourselves that the door we slip through is none other than Jesus Himself!

Tell me, have you ever tried in vain to enter a password to gain access to a site or program online? Right below the box where you're putting in the wrong credentials, there is always an active link you can click immediately that says something like, "Did you forget your password?" Only, more often than not, we ignore that question and waste unnecessary time typing in countless combinations. "Maybe I used this one," we'll muse. When that one doesn't work we say, "Maybe I used that one." We all do it, spinning in circles while the question continues to confront us, "Did you forget your password?"

Likewise, when we're stumbling around in prayer feeling like our words are going nowhere, we desperately need to hear the Spirit of God saying, "Did you forget your password?" When we're circling the room and feeling inadequate in prayer, it's vitally important to remind ourselves that the way we get to God in prayer today, our password if you will, is the same way we were forgiven, restored, and accepted into God's fellowship when we first believed. Same beloved password. Jesus.

Oh, to learn the life-giving skill of poking a stick in our spinning prayer wheels and simply agree with the Spirit! "My password? Why yes, I do seem to have forgotten my password. I'm trying all kinds of ways to get to the throne today and it's Jesus, isn't it? It's always Jesus. It was always Jesus, and it will always be Jesus. You hear me because of Jesus … Thank You, Jesus." Friend, God will open some doors and close others to guide us but the door leading to His presence is always, always open. Praise Jesus. Our strength is learning to make much of Him in prayer.

I've often likened this beautiful prayer habit of making much of Jesus to someone taking the high-occupancy vehicle (HOV) lane on a busy interstate. All the vehicles are going in the same direction, but the HOV lane bypasses the traffic and gets there faster. As believers, we're already in God's presence because of Jesus. *What we're longing for is the conscious awareness of Him.* So start there! Learn to take the HOV lane and "head outta the valley!" Bypass the mental traffic and begin to make much of Jesus. Celebrate His amazing grace. Own your hunger and your neediness. Put words to your desire to grow in your devotion. Choosing to savor the gift of Jesus helps communion begin to flow. Fixing our eyes on Jesus the door, instead of our inabilities and inadequacies, is the way out of our need and into God's abundance. Reaching for Jesus is a fire starter that ignites our hearts and causes them to burn again and again and again!

My friend Mindy and I were talking about being remedial learners and how we are always needing to remind each other of what God has done through Jesus and just how good He is, when Mindy said something so simple and yet so profound. "We have to keep reminding each other because we keep forgetting." Amen, Mindy. And this from my friend Joneal a few days later, on the very same subject: "We just forget to remember, don't we?" So true, Joneal. So very true.

You and I can fan the embers of our prayers by fixing our eyes on the One who lit the flame.

When we're trying to pray and we find ourselves going around in circles, let's *remember not to forget* our password! Let's run for the door that is Jesus the Lord. Anything less will leave us fumbling in the dark.

Hugs,
Shellie

Pray with Me

Dear heavenly Father, we thank You for the gift of Jesus, Your Son and our Savior. We thank You that we are heard through Him. We approach Your throne right now assured that we are warmly welcome and fully accepted because we stand in His favor. Remind us of this, or we will surely forget! The next time we start spinning around in prayer feeling like we are going nowhere fast, bring the truth of Jesus the door back to our hearts and let us slip in and rest in His finished work, trusting that regardless of how we feel, we are being heard because of Jesus! In His name, we pray. Amen.

Practice with Me

Today, let's practice running for the door beyond the parameters of our daily devotion. A sad prophetic verse reads, "*My people have forgotten Me for days without number*" (Jeremiah 2:32). I know that life. I used to live like that between church services. But because I'm tasting the satisfaction of doing life with Him, I now regularly ask Him not to let me forget Him for hours or minutes without number, and He is showing Himself faithful in teaching me how to behold Him throughout the day. We've each been given the amazing ability to hold God in our thoughts and live aware of Him, all through the comings and goings of our busy lives. So, today, every time we realize we're not holding Him in our thoughts and we're no longer listening for Him, regardless of what we're doing at the time, let's run our thirsty souls back to the door that is Jesus Christ our Lord and slip back in, again and again. He is worthy and His presence is life! Pen a line with your intention to learn this never ceasing prayer life below and date it. This is similar to what the Bible calls memorial stones to help people remember a significant event. (See, for example, Joshua 4:6–9.) It gives us an opportunity to note the ways we've seen the Lord move in our lives and share it with our friends and family and generations still to come.

PRAYER HABIT #2

QUIT TRYING TO PRAY IN WAYS YOU DON'T NATURALLY COMMUNICATE.

~HUGS, SHELLIE

2

PERMISSION TO DIGRESS

Habit #2 – Quit trying to pray in ways you don't naturally communicate.

My best friend has called shotgun in the front seat of my ride for countless road trips over the last fifteen to twenty years of my speaking ministry. (I started when I was five. Okay, not really, but I felt like you were doing the math.) More recently, Rhonda and I have found ourselves trying to balance the responsibilities that come with the sandwich generation. Being there for our aging parents while trying our best to keep up with the grandchildren has made it increasingly difficult to sync our travel schedules, but we do our best to keep carving out girlfriend time whenever we can. When we succeed, our catchup conversations are just like our marathon road chats have always been—interesting in an all over the map sort of way. Rhonda and I rarely finish exchanging thoughts on one subject before something is said that makes us jump to another. There's nothing orderly or procedural about our conversation. We'll take a right turn out of one subject to unpack another. We may eventually circle back to readdress an earlier mention, but sometimes threads are simply left hanging.

I'm trying to draw you a picture of what Rhonda and I do when we visit because it's going to help me explain what we don't do, all in the hopes of firmly establishing this chapter's prayer help. In a nutshell: Rhonda and I do not communicate in a linear fashion.

By linear fashion, I mean we don't move from point to point, addressing everything that could be said or needs to be said about the subject on the table before we move on to the next one. Our conversation is neither organized nor monotonous and it doesn't proceed along anything even remotely resembling a straight line. And yet we both feel free to keep talking because we know we're likely to circle back to a previous subject and enlarge upon it during our ongoing conversation. I want to challenge you to think about this because it's how you primarily communicate with flesh and blood people too. Recognizing this and understanding how it applies to our prayer lives can go a long way in helping us learn to enjoy spending time with God.

Random alert. It felt strange typing the name *Rhonda.* I never use my buddy's given name. She was "Red" to everyone who knew her until her grandkids went rogue and christened her "G," for grandmother. She has since become G to me too. By the way, my grandmother name is Keggie, pronounced Keg-E. Dear G has a totally fabricated story about how I got that unique handle. I've lost count of how many times she has entertained a roomful of friends we've just met at a ladies' event or retreat with her tall tale. If you're anything like me, you need to hear that story, if only because I mentioned it.

Here's the short version: G loves to explain how, years ago, back when I was battling an alcohol addiction (which I never have), I fell into a beer keg and almost drowned (which never happened). Insert eye roll from Keggie. I actually got that name many years ago when my nieces and nephews tried to say *Aunt Shellie.* We've never understood how they came up with Aunt Keggie instead, but it stuck, and soon the whole family had shortened it to Keggie. By the time the grandkids came along, they simply followed the rest of the family's lead and adopted Keggie as my grandmother name. That's the real story—but I quickly discovered it was futile to try and counter G's tall tale with the facts because she'd simply respond by soothing me in front of the sweet strangers and saying, "It's okay, Keggie. I'm sure these nice people understand. Besides, you haven't fallen off the wagon in ages!" Over time, I gave up protesting and accepted their well-meaning congratulations on my sobriety. Score one for G.

But I have digressed ... which totally illustrates my point. I digressed because I don't communicate linearly. As I've often confessed to live audiences, I can even digress from my digression. Laugh at me or with me but lean in and hear this. You may not digress as long or as often as I do, but you don't carry on linear conversations with the people in your life either. Test me on this. Ask a friend to join you for coffee and try to be cognizant of how the two of you communicate. Pay attention to how you and your spouse engage and how you and your kids interact. You'll quickly see that you don't stick to a bullet list with any of them!

Now let's apply that to what can happen to us when we set out to pray. Although we don't communicate in a linear straight line fashion during conversation with anyone else, we'll often try to close our eyes and move from point A to point B in a respectful form of prayer that mimics the way we've heard other people pray and conforms to our idea of what prayer should sound like. But because this recitation has no resemblance to any conversation we've ever had or will have with anyone else in our lives, it ends up feeling unfamiliar and awkward and we feel like a failure. Again.

DON'T TALK AT GOD; TALK WITH HIM.

Our intentions are commendable, but there's nothing rewarding about that kind of prayer endeavor. Reciting what we think prayer should sound like instead of simply talking to God leads us from frustration to failure.

And sadly, because the enemy of our souls doesn't play fair, he'll use our sense of defeat to shame us and undermine our good desire to spend time with God, which ends up dissuading us and sending us back to the safety of our list of requests and written prayers ... if we continue at all. And who loses? We do. We lose because itemized lists and recited prayers have none of the ebb and flow of conversation that builds relationship.

I'm not recommending we ramble aimlessly in prayer. You may be thinking Jesus Himself taught us not to babble on like unbelievers, and you would be right! Let's look at that warning from the book of Matthew:

> *And when you pray, do not keep on babbling like pagans, for they think they will be heard because of their many words.*
> (Matthew 6:7 NIV)

As always, context is all important. In the Greco-Roman world of Jesus's day, pagans who worshipped a plethora of false gods believed it was necessary to repeat the same words over and over if they hoped to get their gods' attention. They thought the gods were obligated to hear and respond if they just said the right thing the right way enough times. Of course, we would never do anything like that. Or would we? This is the context that lies at the heart of Jesus's warning not to babble in prayer. He is teaching His followers that prayer is not a recitation of words performed out of a misguided idea that God will hear and respond if we can just say the right thing enough times to tip the scales.

So, no, I'm not suggesting aimless praying either. I am, however, encouraging us to resist the tendency to try and conform to a linear prayer formula. Let's give ourselves permission instead to digress when we're talking with God, to repeat ourselves if we're doing it out of a sincere heart, and to circle back to something we've already covered if our hearts are moved to—all because we're aiming to sit with God and talk to Him, not at Him!

There is no better passage in all of God's Word to look to and try to grasp this than in Jesus's High Priestly Prayer of John 17. As we study this beautiful intimate prayer that Jesus prayed aloud in the hearing of His closest friends in the very best show-and-tell prayer tutorial of all time, I want us to focus on two themes: Jesus's repetition of thought and His expansion of thought. I'm hoping that hearing Jesus talk to His Father without sticking to a linear point-by-point outline will be sweet encouragement to you to do likewise. Jesus opens His prayer by asking the Father to glorify Him so He could glorify the Father:

> *Jesus spoke these words, lifted up His eyes to heaven, and said: "Father, the hour has come.* ***Glorify Your Son, that Your Son also may glorify You.****"* (John 17:1 NKJV)

Only three verses later, after discussing the precious gift of eternal life and the authority His Father has granted Him to give this life to all who believe, Jesus circles back, repeats, and expands upon that initial request for God to glorify Him. Note the similarity between these words and those in verse 1. I've put the repetition and expansion in bold to help you see it:

> *I have glorified You on the earth. I have finished the work which You have given Me to do. And now,* ***O Father, glorify Me together with Yourself, with the glory which I had with You before the world was.*** (John 17:4–5 NKJV)

That repetition isn't the exception in this prayer either. Jesus repeats Himself and expands on requests and observations throughout it! In John 17:6–19, as He prays for His disciples, He asks the Father to keep them from the evil one, to make their joy complete, and to sanctify them. Then in verse 20, He circles back and broadens the scope of those petitions by saying, *"I do not pray for these alone, but also for those who will believe in Me through their word."*

That's us, friends! Jesus circled back in prayer for us! Did He forget us the first time? Of course not. We've never been an afterthought, and we never will be. Savor these words from Psalm 139:13–18 (NIV):

> *For you created my inmost being; you knit me together in my mother's womb. I praise you because I am fearfully and wonderfully made; your works are wonderful, I know that full well. My frame was not hidden from you when I was made in the secret place, when I was woven together in the depths of the earth. Your eyes saw my unformed body; all the days ordained for me were written in your book before one of them came to be. How precious to me are your thoughts, God! How vast is the sum of them! Were I to count them, they would outnumber the grains of sand—when I awake, I am still with you.*

Need more convincing? Here's another example of pure repetition in Jesus's High Priestly Prayer. In verse 14, Jesus asks the Father to keep His followers because they are not of this world, and in verse 16, He makes the same request, using the same words. Again, I've put the repetition in bold:

> *But now I come to You, and these things I speak in the world, that they may have My joy fulfilled in themselves. I have given them Your word; and the world has hated them because* ***they are not of the world, just as I am not of the world****. I do not pray that You should take them out of the world, but that You should keep them from the evil one.* ***They are not of the world, just as I am not of the world.***
>
> (John 17:13–15 NKJV)

And then, as He closes His prayer, He takes joy in the disciples' faith once again, saying, "*O righteous Father! The world has not known You, but I have known You; and* ***these have known that You***

sent me" (John 17:25 NKJV). Savor that. Sweet Jesus, celebrating their belief in Him again. I know how powerless our prayers can sound to our own ears. Let this word minister to you. God takes joy in the faith we're demonstrating as we call out to Him!

The lessons offered by Jesus's prayer tutorial are pure gold for anyone serious about learning how to keep company with God, but one of my favorite moments is found earlier in the chapter. I've saved it for last because it's so dear to me. Heads up, I'll need to digress in the middle of it.

In John 17:8 (NKJV), we're blessed to overhear Jesus exulting over His disciples with these words: *"For I have given to them the words which You have given Me; and they have received them, and have known surely that I came forth from You; and they have believed that You sent Me."*

It's fortifying food for my soul that Jesus doesn't include a caveat here of all the times the disciples didn't get it right, didn't keep His Word, and failed to completely understand that He was speaking as God Himself to them! Jesus simply speaks of the followers His Father gave Him as having faith in Him and His words, without once revisiting their past mistakes. Oh, the grace! He was owning their good faith even as He was praying for their ongoing sanctification (a big word that describes the process of spiritual growth). For someone who falls forward in my pursuit of Jesus more than I would like to admit, that's really good news.

And get this, Jesus says they *"surely"* believed even though they had just recently confessed in John 16:30, *"Now we know that You know all things, and that You have no need for anyone to question You; this is why we believe that You came forth from God."* Now? Now they believed?! After walking with Him for three plus years? After seeing one miracle after another and listening to sermon after sermon? Yes and yes, and yet, Jesus passes right over the timing of their declaration and takes joy in the disciples' growing faith. That both amazes and encourages me to press on toward the goal of knowing God. Our faith and our prayers, as feeble and weak as we may think them to be, can give God joy and satisfaction too!

Is that a foreign thought to you? Have you ever allowed yourself to even consider that your God loves to hear you pray? Or are you prone to acting like God is grading your effort and you're not making the grade? Both my years in ministry and the real-time feedback I hear when I speak on prayer tell me the answer is B. It makes me sad, but infinitely more important, I believe it grieves our good Father.

Savor these words from Proverbs 15:8, "*The sacrifice of the wicked is an abomination to the* L*ORD*, *but the prayer of the upright is His delight.*" That's just one of the places in Scripture that shows God taking satisfaction in our prayers—and that includes your prayers and mine, not just hers. And because I'm not ignorant of the enemy's devices (see 2 Corinthians 2:11), let me address "*the prayer of the upright*" for anyone questioning whether they qualify for such a description. Upright doesn't mean sinless. Without grace and the finished work of the cross, none of us could ever be sinless. In Christ Jesus, however, we are upright and righteous.

> *For He made Him who knew no sin to be sin for us, that we might become the righteousness of God in Him.*
>
> (2 Corinthians 5:21 NKJV)

So hello, upright believer, God loves to hear from you, but I've wandered a good ways from the main point of giving ourselves permission to digress, so let's recap as we close this chapter.

I'm hoping these examples of Jesus repeating Himself and expanding on earlier thoughts as He spoke to His Father will give you fresh encouragement to sit with God, open your heart, and simply talk to Him. When we allow ourselves to reach for God in prayer without berating ourselves for getting off point, when we experience the freedom found in not trying to pray in a straight line from subject A to subject B, when we give ourselves the joy of sitting to talk with God and not at Him, we position ourselves to linger with Him. And in lingering, we begin to taste the sweet nectar of His company. This is where so many amazing dividends start presenting themselves. We begin to enjoy our time with God, we grow hungry for more, and our growing satisfaction in prayer brings us back to God over and again. For in His presence, our desires begin to change, and no one is more amazed than we are.

Let's stop evaluating and micromanaging our prayers and try talking to God instead. Just talk, the way you would talk with any other friend, only this is the Friend "*who sticks closer than a brother*" (Proverbs 18:24).

Hugs,
Shellie

Pray with Me

Dear heavenly Father, we long to commune with You in prayer and yet our inability to focus can make us feel like such failures. Help us learn to sit with You and talk to You without being tripped up by critiquing our own prayer words. We know that it isn't the number of words we use or the way we use them that move You. Your desire is for our fellowship and our desire is for Yours. Help us get out of our own way so we can enjoy You. In the sweet name of Jesus, we pray. Amen.

Practice with Me

Today, let's practice having a running conversation with our Father that is nonlinear and open-ended. Let's give ourselves permission to start and stop a prayer, pause a prayer, or pick a prayer back up wherever we were praying when we got interrupted or distracted by life and all of its joys and sorrows, demands and opportunities. I encourage you to start a line of prayer here in the space I've provided. It's more than okay if you don't *finish* it; this time, it's actually recommended. It will help cement this prayer principle. We're not aiming to write an essay with a brilliant open and impressive close. If you have your book with you and you want to come back and add to it later, that's fine but it's not necessary. You can resume praying whenever and wherever. The Lord never loses the thread of conversation. Praise Him!

PRAYER HABIT #3

WHEN YOUR MIND WANDERS IN PRAYER, SIMPLY BRING IT BACK.

~HUGS, SHELLIE

3

THOSE WHO WANDER ARE STILL WELCOME

Habit #3 – When your mind wanders in prayer, simply bring it back.

I was deep in prayer one morning over a serious concern that was causing my immediate family great anxiety. I'd been asking the Lord to calm everyone's spirits and help us rest in Him when I heard myself say something that was so completely ridiculous, I didn't know whether to laugh out loud or watch for incoming lightning strikes! My exact words are lost to memory, but it was something like, "Dear Lord, I am Your peace." I know, right?! I am God's peace? For goodness' sake, I was appealing to the Prince of Peace Himself!

> *For unto us a child is born, to us a son is given; and the government shall be upon his shoulder, and his name shall be called Wonderful Counselor, Mighty God, Everlasting Father, Prince of Peace.* (Isaiah 9:6 ESV)

And here I was telling Him that little old me was His peace. Yikes! The truth is, it's not always comforting to know God sees our hearts and reads our thoughts before the words are on our lips. (See Psalm 139:4.) Amen? This, however, was one of those times when I was sure glad He did. I knew God understood I was needing Him to soothe our souls and show us the way forward. I was equally convinced He knew my intentions were to say, "*You* are *our* peace!" I was still mortified.

Had I thought hiding from the Almighty were possible (it's not; see Psalm 139), I would've crawled under the porch swing. My gaffe would have been sacrilegious if it were intentional, but it wasn't. The problem? My mind had drifted off somewhere after I said the words, "Dear Lord." I wish I could tell you this is unusual and it's not likely to happen again, but I can't, and it will.

In the last chapter, we explored the natural rhythms of everyday conversation. We noted that we don't communicate with other people in step-by-step essay style, staying on point from start to finish without once straying from the original subject. We compared that with how we often try to talk to God in a vastly different point-by-point, linear mode of communication that's wholly unfamiliar and one we never use with anyone else at any time in our lives. The contrast helped us see why we can get so frustrated in prayer and feel like such failures. Remember? Well, the focus of this chapter is similar but stay with me and I think you'll see why I felt like it deserved its own conversation. That opening story, as embarrassing as it is, felt like a good place to open our discussion.

Though God's companionship has indeed become life to me, I can still be deep in prayer one minute—invested in sweet heavenly communion and enjoying it immensely—only to find my thoughts meandering a country mile the next. To be clear, I can wander so far off the prayer path that once I realize it's happening, again, I can't remember what I was praying about when I left the track! Sigh. If I were trying to set myself up as an expert on prayer in these early pages, this would be last thing I would admit to you, but I have no such aspirations. I'm eager to share my experiences with you, even an embarrassing one that features my wandering thoughts and questionable prayer, because of what I've learned in my pursuit of a deeper relationship with God. I believe the things the Lord has taught me can help *you* build a stronger prayer life too! And that's my goal, not empty notoriety. Besides, you get me, don't you? Squirrel chasers unite.

Before I share with you what the Lord has taught me to do in these moments, I'd like to describe what used to happen once I realized my thoughts had strayed during prayer yet again, despite my best efforts to reign them in. Guilt and shame would jump on me as surely as the sun rises in the east and sets in the west. I'd swallow the enemy's accusations that my prayers were pitiful and powerless, and I'd have the most frustrating experience settling back into prayer, if indeed I could. More times than not, I'd give up and come away from my prayer time feeling like a total failure, even though I desperately wanted to experience the relationship with God, through Christ, that was promised to me in His Word! Ugh. That's the type of vivid memory that leads me to write as transparently as I can. Guilt and shame are some of the devil's most effective tools against believers who long for intimacy in prayer but find themselves trapped in cycles of defeat instead. I need you to hear me on this. They don't have to be.

We can take those weapons and many others out of the enemy's ugly hands by running to God with our challenges and weaknesses and watching Him work with what we bring to Him. I know this by experience. My mind still wanders in prayer on days that end in *y*, but it no longer defeats me because I've learned what to do about it and I'm about to share two of my secrets with you. Are you ready for the first one?

When your mind wanders, bring it back.

That's it. That's the whole tip. If your thoughts wander ten times, bring them back eleven. His Presence is worth every reach we make toward Him! You're probably thinking that's entirely too simple but hear me on this. That is the very attitude tripping us up! We act like prayer is a complicated discipline we have to get just right to please our Father and it's all on us to do it well. Wrong. Prayer is less about doing and more about being—being with God.

Distraction can't disqualify you in prayer because it was never your focus that qualified you! And it never will be either. Our access to the throne is and will always be our belief in Jesus and His finished work on the cross that grants redemption to all who believe and reconciliation with God. Which brings me to something else I discovered about my tendency to wander off the prayer path.

WANDERING THOUGHTS CAN ACTUALLY BE A BLESSING IN DISGUISE IF WE EXPLORE THEM WITH GOD.

Perhaps you're familiar with the line J.R.R. Tolkien penned in *Lord of the Rings*, "Not all those who wander are lost."[2] I've always liked the quote because I love a good wandering road trip. Taking the road less traveled, seeing things I didn't anticipate and couldn't have seen had I journeyed in a straight line—this speaks to my adventure-loving soul. It's all the better if I'm with someone whose company I enjoy along the way.

I've come to think of prayer like that. I'm definitely not recommending the mental wool-gathering that led to the embarrassing "I am Your peace" prayer I confessed to earlier. But borrowing heavily from Tolkien here, I've come to believe not all wandering prayers are wasted.

Consider the Psalms. Many of them are the recorded prayers of earnest believers and boy, oh boy, do they ever wander! Psalm 55 records one such prayer by David, the shepherd boy who became a king. You remember David, right? He's the one the Bible calls the "*man after* [God's] *own heart*" (1 Samuel 13:14). Many commentators believe David is talking in this psalm about the betrayal of his close friend and advisor, Ahithophel, and the subsequent rebellion of his son, Absalom. Few are the wounds that cut as deeply

---

2. J.R.R. Tolkien, *Lord of the Rings, Part 1: The Fellowship of the Ring* (London: Harper Collins, 1993), 186.

as those that come from friends and family. Buckle up and let's work our way through this messy psalm. There are some valuable takeaways waiting for us.

David opens his prayer with an address to God before launching directly into a full-scale lament about his enemies:

> *Listen to my prayer, God; and do not hide Yourself from my pleading. Give Your attention to me and answer me; I am restless in my complaint and severely distracted, because of the voice of the enemy, because of the pressure of the wicked; for they bring down trouble upon me and in anger they hold a grudge against me.* (Psalm 55:1–3)

In the next few verses, David is going to double down on his complaints, but if we pay attention, we'll see something interesting happening. As he continues to pray, David appears to start dialoguing more with his own thoughts rather than praying. I can do that! How about you? In verse 6, he even quotes himself, almost as if he is remembering something he has said to another person.

> *My heart is in anguish within me, and the terrors of death have fallen upon me. Fear and trembling come upon me, and horror has overwhelmed me. I said, "Oh, that I had wings like a dove! I would fly away and be at rest. Behold, I would flee far away, I would spend my nights in the wilderness. Selah. I would hurry to my place of refuge from the stormy wind and heavy gale."* (Psalm 55:4–8)

Having done a bit of daydreaming about flying far, far away, David will bring himself back to prayer in the next section. Only this time, we get to watch as he makes his case for God to intervene by providing a detailed description of his enemies' sins—you know, just in case God Almighty has missed them.

> *Confuse them, Lord, divide their tongues, for I have seen violence and strife in the city. Day and night they go around her upon her walls, and evil and harm are in her midst.*

> *Destruction is in her midst; oppression and deceit do not depart from her streets.* (Psalm 55:9–11)

Now, this is where studying the structure of David's prayer gets really interesting. He is going to drift back into his earlier thoughts about the unfairness of the situation. Perhaps rehashing his litany of complaints stirred him up again? Maybe. Notice the shift in the following verses as David begins to dwell once again on how betrayed he feels.

> *For it is not an enemy who taunts me, then I could endure it; nor is it one who hates me who has exalted himself against me, then I could hide myself from him. But it is you, a man my equal, my companion and my confidant; we who had sweet fellowship together, walked in the house of God among the commotion.* (Psalm 55:12–14)

Did you see it? David said, "*It is you, a man my equal.*" Wait. What's happening now? Is David speaking to his betrayer? I thought he was praying. Is his enemy there, listening to him? Possibly, but probably not. It seems more likely that David has left off praying and slipped into his own thoughts again. Just like we do! He's about to bring them back to God again, and we can learn to do the same!

This time, David makes it clear that he wants God to stick it to his enemies, big time.

> *May death come deceitfully upon them; may they go down alive to Sheol, for evil is in their dwelling, in their midst.* (Psalm 55:15)

Whoa! "Let death come upon them" is an example of an imprecatory prayer, one in which someone calls down curses or calamity on those perceived to be their enemy or an enemy of God. There are other examples of this type of prayer in God's Word. Theologians are divided over whether the Bible is condoning these "get 'em, God!" prayers or if the Word is simply recording the depth of our human emotions and our capacity for revenge.

I'll tell you where I land on it. I can't find any scriptural instruction to pray down curses or calamities on our enemies, but I can find plenty of verses that teach us to do just the opposite. I'm not confident I know when to use an imprecatory prayer and when not to, but I know it's safe to pattern myself after Jesus Himself who said, "*You have heard that it was said, 'You shall love your neighbor and hate your enemy.' But I say to you, Love your enemies and pray for those who persecute you, so that you may be sons of your Father who is in heaven*" (Matthew 5:43–45 ESV).

Regardless, David doesn't stay with his death wish request any longer than he did with any of the other wandering prayers that preceded it. Instead, David's next words give us yet another peek into what he has concluded from musing over the entire situation. Suddenly, he is back to being David, the man after God's own heart.

> *As for me, I shall call upon God, and the LORD will save me. Evening and morning and at noon, I will complain and moan, and He will hear my voice. He will redeem my soul in peace from the battle which is against me, for they are many who are aggressive toward me. God will hear and humiliate them—even the one who sits enthroned from ancient times—Selah. . . . Cast your burden upon the LORD and He will sustain you; He will never allow the righteous to be shaken.*
>
> (Psalm 55:16–19, 22)

Side note? I find it fascinating that David says he will complain and murmur in the very same breath he uses to announce that he will call on God and God will save him. It tells me God can handle all of our big emotions. He gave them to us and the more of our real selves we bring to Him, the more of His very real presence we can experience! We'll come back to this thought in a later chapter. For now, let's note one final mood swing. After making a beautiful declaration of his trust in God to hear him, answer him, and sustain him, David closes his wandering prayer with one last thought and surprise—it has more of that "get 'em, God" tone.

But You, God, will bring them down to the pit of destruction;
men of bloodshed and deceit will not live out half their days.
But I will trust in You. (Psalm 55:23)

Dizzy much? David was all over the place, right? And yet God chose to include David's prayer in His Word. Sit with that a moment. God recorded David's scattered, rambling, and disorganized prayer for all of time, and we can be so glad He did. There's much to be learned from David's dialogue.

Remember when I said prayer is about being with God, and our wandering thoughts can be a blessing *if* we explore them with God? David just perfectly illustrated both of those points. As David processed with prayer, we get to see:

1. David talking to God and David talking to himself.
2. David thinking about his problem, commiserating with himself over it, and then reevaluating the situation in light of what he knew about God.
3. Finally, we get to witness David finding the strength to renew his faith in God being with him in the trial, recommitting himself to trusting God, and returning to God in prayer again.

What I want us to see is how David found his way back to trusting God by bringing Him his whole heart and openly sharing everything on his mind. David didn't self-edit his prayers, and he didn't let his wandering thoughts keep him from continuing to seek His Father's face.

Let's apply this to our own prayer lives. Oftentimes we'll set out to pray and our minds will wander off and begin offering us situations we don't want to think about, grievances we think we shouldn't dwell on, and feelings we shouldn't have. Sound familiar? How many times do we try to stuff down and ignore those persistent thoughts in a sincere but misguided effort to stay on track in prayer, when what we really need is to process them with *the* problem solver, the lover of our souls? Let's learn from David.

We can ask Holy Spirit to help us explore our feelings with God instead of accepting another prayer defeat. If we process with God and make room for Him to shine much-needed light, give us direction, and bring us peace, our little prayer *detours* can become that day's living bread.

GOD CAN USE OUR DETOURS FOR DIRECTION!

Here's something ironic for you: I've found that we have to be intentional about setting aside time to be with God, and we have to be just as intentional about not micromanaging and structuring that time.

When we learn to quit performing our prayers, we discover just how much we're beginning to enjoy simply being with God. These days, I refuse to accept condemnation when my mind wanders. I simply bring it back, ask the Lord to help me focus, and start again. If it persistently wanders back to that one thing like it's an elephant in the room between us, I figure there's something there I need to stop and address. Afterward, if I can't remember what I was praying about before the detour, I tell the Lord that too. I think He laughs with me even as I resume my praise, open another line of conversation, or lift up another need. And here's the kicker! Learning not to feel guilty about my mind wandering has meant I stay in prayer longer and when I stay in prayer longer, I get to enjoy God's presence more, which makes me want to return to prayer again and again. That's the most victorious win/win I can imagine, and I want you to know it too.

Hugs,
Shellie

Pray with Me

Dear heavenly Father, help us quit thinking of prayer as something we have to do just right for it to be pleasing to You and beneficial for us. It almost sounds too good to be true that You simply want to hear from us. Help us break the habit of continuously self-editing our prayers and thinking we are or aren't accomplishing something and learn instead to listen for You and respond to You. And when our minds wander, teach us to bring them back, because You know the more time we spend talking with You, the more we'll enjoy talking with You! In the unparalleled name of Jesus, we pray. Amen.

Practice with Me

Let's bring something to the Lord in prayer that's weighing on us. I'm talking about that thing that's dominating our thought lives and threatening our peace. Use the space provided below to begin praying about it. (Write in code if it's a private matter you don't want anyone else to find.) Now, ask the Lord for help with it. Ask for direction, comfort, provision, whatever you feel like you need and then wait for Him to respond. Pay attention to where your thoughts go while you're waiting. If your mind doesn't wander, say hallelujah and give thanks! However, if your mind does wander to another issue, repeatedly, make it a prayer too while looking for any possible connection. If you don't see a relationship between the two, that's okay! If you feel led (and you can remember where you were), go back to the initial request and finish praying and listening. The goal is learning not to feel guilty for your wandering thoughts and let them push you out of prayer! Instead, practice this requesting, resting, and returning. (I have three Rs to help you remember!) It's a sweet rhythm that will encourage your prayer life, and on the authority of God's Word, I can assure you He's waiting for you in it.

PRAYER HABIT #4

DON'T FORGET TO LEAN ON THE TEAM.

~HUGS, SHELLIE

4

SURROUNDED BY SUPERSTARS

Habit #4 – Don't forget to lean on the Team.

It happened again. One minute I was googling to find out which sport was the least popular one on television to make a point about something I can no longer remember because the next minute, I was knee deep in learning about the sport of ferret-legging and I couldn't quit clicking on informative articles. I'm sure you can relate. Perhaps you've never gotten caught up researching ferret-legging, but I'm sure you've fallen down Internet holes a time or two yourself. As eager as I am to get into the meat of this chapter, if you'll indulge me, I'd like to share my newly acquired education first, if only because I've learned so many fun facts.

We'll need to make sure everyone understands what ferrets are before we begin. This is one of those chocolate and vanilla situations. Depending on who you ask, ferrets are either small, sharp-teethed, vicious carnivores eager to maim you, or adorable, fun-loving pets capable of responding to human affection. Either way, would you be willing to tie the bottoms of your pants legs up, loose two live ferrets into your trousers, secure your belt, and compete with fellow ferret leggers to see who can best endure the ensuing chaos? Nor would I, but those are the rules of this bizarre sport that is said to have originated in England centuries ago. The competition is held before a judge who determines which competitor holds out the longest before releasing the animals from his britches. (My southern family has long used the word britches for pants. I've never used it in a manuscript but somehow it just feels right here.) The last man standing as the ferrets get increasingly frantic about escaping is henceforth declared the big winner. (I couldn't make this up if I tried.) As recently as 2009, national ferret-legging events were still being held stateside, but these days, ferret-legging is being described as a dying sport, which is weird because it sounds like so much fun.

If my editor hasn't edited this opening out of existence, and on the outside chance you're interested in starting a ferret-legging league in your hometown, here are more of the rules. You can't compete under the influence of alcohol or drugs, and neither can your ferrets. (Bless the ferrets.) Also, the ferrets must have all of their original teeth and filing down or blunting their teeth will get you disqualified. Apparently, a female version of this sport, in which the ferrets were put in the ladies' blouses, never gained any steam. That proves nothing about anything and I'm not smiling, you're smiling.

To my knowledge, no one in my family, male or female, has ever engaged in ferret-legging, and that's saying something. We're a sports-loving, highly competitive bunch of people. If we're not playing sports, we're watching them. Sports analogies come natural to us. And while segueing into a prayer discussion from ferret-legging is going to be unusual, even for me, I'm game to try. (See what I did there? I'm almost a professional.)

Here's some great news! Prayer isn't a last man or last woman standing type of endeavor where the judge just might rule in our favor *if* we manage to persevere long enough under less than favorable conditions. We Bible believers know this on a conscious level. But what happens when we take our God-hungry selves to prayer, eager to spend time with the Father, and He feels distant again.

And we're surprised again? I know this one. I'll tell you what can happen with me.

Even though I know differently, I can still find myself slipping into old habits and acting like prayer is an individual sport, sheer endurance is necessary, and it's all up to me, myself, and I to stay in it to win it. Knuckle down, Shellie. E for effort and all of the other clichés. Ugh. That's a lot of transparency for someone writing a prayer book but do stay with me. I'm getting to the glorious part I want you to apply to your prayer life!

See, I'm learning what to do when I realize I'm struggling and striving for God's attention again as if it is all up to me to pray, and the discovery has been a game-changer. It's also so elementary, I feel a little silly writing it down, but it has meant so much to me that I'm choosing to trust God can use my words to help someone else. So here's the tip: *I simply stop and remind myself that I'm not alone in prayer.* My lakeside neighbors may look out their windows and see me sitting on the dock alone. All the world may see me and think I am isolated. I may even feel like I'm all by myself. But if we could peel back the curtains of this world long enough to glimpse what is really happening, we would see that I'm actually surrounded by a crowd. Let's do a little roll call and see who's present.

To begin with, my early morning prayer meeting is being attended by none other than the Holy Trinity, and whenever you bow your sweet head to pray, you are enjoying the same miraculous privilege. As the apostle Paul wrote in 2 Corinthians 13:14 (NIV), *"May the grace of the Lord Jesus Christ, and the love of God, and the fellowship of the Holy Spirit be with you all."* That, my friend, is the most supportive and loving team of all time. Cherish this thought, friend. God wouldn't ask us to pray if He didn't intend to listen.

We're not lonesome individuals calling out to a faraway Being, hopelessly limited by our own ability—or should I say *inability?*—to communicate, and we're not desperately hoping to say the right words to be heard. We have the full support of the supernatural team of Father, Son, and Holy Spirit. Their power is out of this world and they're ready and willing to assist us in prayer.

> *Now in the same way the Spirit also helps our weakness; for we do not know what to pray for as we should, but the Spirit Himself intercedes for us with groanings too deep for words; and He who searches the hearts knows what the mind of the Spirit is, because He intercedes for the saints according to the will of God. And we know that God causes all things to work together for good to those who love God, to those who are called according to His purpose.* (Romans 8:26–28)

I've discovered my spirit will often start settling into prayer once I begin acknowledging the manifold work of the Trinity. I rarely use the same words, but here's the gist of what that looks like. I begin to thank God for choosing me to be in relationship with Him from the foundation of the world and for the gift of His Son, my Redeemer. (See Ephesians 1:4–6.) I express my gratitude to Jesus for going to the cross and accomplishing the sacred work that made it possible. (See John 3:16). And I thank Holy Spirit for doing life with me and teaching me what is mine in Christ Jesus so I can enjoy my inheritance! (See John 14:26.) This is the all-powerful divine quorum with us in prayer, but we have still more otherworldly prayer pals attending our devotions.

The believers who have gone on before us are also witnessing our efforts and keeping us company. We can find the author of the book of Hebrews celebrating the biographies of Old Testament saints in a passage that is known as the hall of faith. As we read about their exploits, let's keep in mind that the people being described here led flesh and blood lives on planet earth, just like us. I encourage you to read this chapter in its entirety. For now, we'll jump into the middle of this fascinating passage and begin reading in Hebrews 11:32–40:

> *And what more shall I say? For time will fail me if I tell of Gideon, Barak, Samson, Jephthah, of David and Samuel and*

the prophets, who by faith conquered kingdoms, performed acts of righteousness, obtained promises, shut the mouths of lions, quenched the power of fire, escaped the edge of the sword, from weakness were made strong, became mighty in war, put foreign armies to flight. Women received back their dead by resurrection; and others were tortured, not accepting their release, so that they might obtain a better resurrection; and others experienced mocking and flogging, and further, chains and imprisonment. They were stoned, they were sawn in two, they were tempted, they were put to death with the sword; they went about in sheepskins, in goatskins, being destitute, afflicted, tormented (people of whom the world was not worthy), wandering in deserts, on mountains, and sheltering in caves and holes in the ground. And all these, having gained approval through their faith, did not receive what was promised, because God had provided something better for us, so that apart from us they would not be made perfect.

Hebrews 12:1–2 continues:

Therefore, since we also have such a great cloud of witnesses surrounding us, let's rid ourselves of every obstacle and the sin which so easily entangles us, and let's run with endurance the race that is set before us, looking only at Jesus, the originator and perfecter of the faith, who for the joy set before Him endured the cross, despising the shame, and has sat down at the right hand of the throne of God.

That crowd of witnesses surrounding us isn't made up of wannabe optimists wearing rose-colored glasses. These are fellow believers who fought the good fight and now they're cheering you and me on from heaven! Try to imagine their perspective as they watch us pursuing God. They lived faithful heroic lives, enduring everything we read about—and they did it in shadow of the cross, believing in the promise, but without the ever-present help of the indwelling Holy Spirit. I imagine them shouting words of encouragement. "You can do it! Lean on Jesus. He's with you!" This crowd of witnesses makes me want to press on in this high calling and make full use of my new covenant privileges! I hope it does the same for you, but I'm not through. There's more.

In addition to the Holy Trinity and the cloud of witnesses who have gone before us, we have yet another layer of supernatural prayer aid. Somehow, in ways too wonderful for me to grasp, saints who are still living and breathing on this side of heaven are also joined with us as we bow our heads to God, even when we're physically separated and even if we've never actually met in real time! Scripture tells us we're all seated together in the Spirit, regardless of the distance between us on earth.

> *But God, being rich in mercy, because of His great love with which He loved us, even when we were dead in our wrongdoings, made us alive together with Christ (by grace you have been saved), and raised us up with Him, and seated us with Him in the heavenly places in Christ Jesus.*
>
> (Ephesians 2:4–6)

You and I sit together in heavenly places. That's beautiful. Tell me, how many times have you met a fellow believer for the first time and yet within minutes, you began to feel like you've known the other person forever? It's happened to me more times than I can count, and I believe it's because we've been worshipping and praying together beyond earth's veil. Oh, that we would grasp the enormous potential of uniting with other believers on this side!

Our culture has a mindset of hearty individualism. We celebrate the concept of digging deep and relying on one's own efforts to survive whatever challenges stand in the way. Whether the playing field is an actual one in a sports venue, or the hypothetical race we see ourselves competing in across every other area of our lives, we're used to prioritizing our own goals and growth over the group's advancement as we try to prove our own worth.

We've been steeped in this winner-take-all mentality that encourages us to compete, compare, evaluate, and measure our success against the gains of everyone around us. As deeply enshrined as this posture is in our society, the body of Christ must surrender it to thrive as members of a kingdom that operates under vastly different rules. When we think of prayer as strictly our individual response to God, we forego the vitally important strength and support we're meant to enjoy as members of Christ's body. We diminish the community of believers when we're called to be catalysts to one another's faith. In Christ, independence isn't a characteristic to be celebrated; it's disobedience!

THE ENEMY OF YOUR SOUL WANTS YOU TO PRAY IN ISOLATION. DON'T FALL FOR IT!

Several years ago, I became intrigued with how often the apostle Paul thanked God for the faith of other believers and prayed for them. Paul is often quoted saying things like, *"For this reason I too, having heard of the faith in the Lord Jesus which exists among you and your love for all the saints, do not cease giving thanks for you, while making mention of you in my prayers; that the God of our Lord Jesus Christ, the Father of glory, may give you a spirit of wisdom and of revelation in the knowledge of Him"* (Ephesians 1:15–17).

One morning, while considering this appreciation and love for the body of Christ that Paul modeled, a question settled in my heart. I knew God put it there. *"Can you imagine what it would be like if you didn't know any other Christians, and you were trying to follow Christ all by yourself?"* That one question—and the realization of how incredibly hard it would be to walk this faith journey alone—forever impacted my appreciation for the body of Christ. It caused me to express my gratitude for other believers and pray for them more often. And because God is a win/win Father, it added another layer of intimacy to my prayer life.

We need to share our prayer requests. We need to treasure the body of Christ and bring our brothers' and sisters' needs to the throne. And when we pray, we need to take strength in knowing we aren't the sole survivor calling out to God from a deserted island. (Or the last ferret legger standing!) We're making our appeals to God the Father, through Christ Jesus the Son, by the Holy Spirit, attended by those who have gone before us, asking alongside the worldwide church we cannot see! Let's live reminding ourselves of this beautiful truth whenever we bow to pray: *We're never less alone than when we're alone with God.*

The cross of Christ was God's forever demonstration that He reaches first. He stretched His arms out for us, long before we ever considered reaching for Him.

> *Blessed be the God and Father of our Lord Jesus Christ, who has blessed us with every spiritual blessing in the heavenly places in Christ, just as He chose us in Him before the foundation of the world, that we would be holy and blameless before Him. In love He predestined us to adoption as sons and daughters through Jesus Christ to Himself, according to the good pleasure of His will, to the praise of the glory of His grace, with which He favored us in the Beloved.*
>
> (Ephesians 1:3–6)

God is still loving first, and He is still reaching first. We were all lost and alone and without hope in this world before He made the first move. (See Ephesians 2:12.) Every single time we stretch our hands toward Him, every single time we look for Him, we're responding to Him calling to us. We simply don't have it in us to make the first step. Every move we make toward Him is a response to His kind invitation to come. You're reading this book because you want to learn to pray, right? So be encouraged by the truth that your desire to connect with God in prayer came from God's heart first. Our longing to spend time with this faithful God who loves us is and always will be eclipsed by His desire for our fellowship, and He has set us up for success.

Rely on the supernatural team of Father, Son, and Holy Spirit. Lean on the body of believers walking with you on planet earth. Be encouraged by the great cloud of witnesses who have gone before us and enjoy the win!

Hugs,
Shellie

Pray with Me

Dear heavenly Father, we're forgetful and we need Your help. Whenever we're sitting in prayer feeling alone and acting like it is up to us to pray in a way that gets Your attention, would You please remind us that we already have it! Help us to remember that You reach first. You always have and You always will. Every grasp we make toward You, desiring to know You, is a response to Your holy invitation to be known. Thank You for choosing us! Thank You, Jesus, for making a way for us to be with You. Thank You, Holy Spirit, for dwelling with us! Together, You are Immanuel, the Triune God who is with us, and it is in the unparalleled name of Jesus that we pray, grateful for all that You are and all You have done. Amen.

Practice with Me

Spend a few minutes jotting down the names of people who have inspired, taught, mentored, or prayed for you in the space provided. You might even think of someone who checks all of those boxes. Maybe someone comes to mind who was instrumental to you coming to faith. Perhaps that person has gone on to heaven, but others have since come alongside you to encourage you in your journey. Let's practice availing ourselves of Team Jesus today by praying for these people and then reaching out to them with a note of appreciation. We can be the good team members we want to have by sending them a thank-you text or (gasp!) actually giving them a call. I'm old enough to remember when the devices on our hips and in our purses were phones. Influence can be an overused word in our culture these days, but you and I can be true influencers by intentionally pursuing meaningful communication that encourages each other and advances the kingdom.

PRAYER HABIT #5

TAKE A NOTE TO FREE YOUR MIND

~HUGS, SHELLIE

5

FOR THOSE OF US WHO FORGET TO REMEMBER

Habit #5 – Take a note to free your mind!

Have we established that I'm selectively forgetful? I think I mentioned it in passing, but I'm not sure you understand the scope of the situation. I refer to myself as selectively forgetful because I can forget to remember very important details while retaining totally inconsequential facts from my grade school years that benefit exactly no one. My selective forgetfulness is involuntary. It's also legendary in my circle of family and friends. How about a story break for illustration?

I was speaking at a large conference with a number of other speakers on the program. Many of these events have a countdown clock at the back of the venue to help all the speakers stay on schedule, but during mic check, I had noticed this particular gathering wasn't making use of one. Being fully aware that I can get passionate about my message and lose track of time, I decided to enlist my friend's help.

Rhonda agreed to position herself to my immediate left in the front row of the large auditorium, ready to flash me our predetermined signal. (Yes, this is "road trip Rhonda" from chapter 2, aka "Red," aka "G.") The plan was for Rhonda to catch my eye and casually lift her hand, palm facing me, in a *wrap it up soon* reminder when I had about five minutes left in my allotted time. If I were going strong, this would be my cue to settle down and begin closing. Doesn't that sound like a fine idea? It should have been.

Sometime later, I was speaking to the assembled believers, knee deep in making much of Jesus and unpacking the beauty of His Word while throwing in the occasional funny story because that's how I roll. I was fully enjoying every minute of it when I caught Rhonda waving to me out of the corner of my eye. Unfortunately, a bit of time had passed between the formation of our plan and my spot on the program. Enough time, apparently, for me to totally forget about our agreed-upon sign. I couldn't believe Rhonda was waving at me in front of this large crowd during such an important moment. Did she not realize I was trying to focus?!

I smiled in Rhonda's direction and continued with my point. She waved again. I was incredulous! I was trying to stay on message, but I was silently thinking, "Really, Red? Can't you see I'm busy here?" And that's when Rhonda moved her hand to her throat and made a not-so-subtle slicing motion. Oh! Right. I may be forgetful but I'm reasonably intelligent. I wrapped up quickly. So what does my impressive forgetfulness have to do with prayer? A lot actually! I've learned to enjoy prayer in spite of the way my brain operates, and I think what I've learned can help you too. I'm excited to explain.

As soon as I sit down to pray, all the things I need to remember not to forget start racing through my head. It happens all the time and I've talked to enough of you across the body of Christ to know it's not just me. If it's not the enemy trying to goad us out of prayer by reminding us of all the things we could be doing and should be doing (we'll get to his devilish distractions in a coming chapter), it's our own busy little multitasking minds spitting out an endless list of things we can't afford to forget! And right now, I'm not talking about those trivial distractions we can afford to wave away. I'm talking about the important, time-sensitive things that don't need to fall through the cracks. What do we do about those?

I used to think I had two choices. One, I could try not to think about that critical to-do list and keep my mind on what I was praying about, hoping I wouldn't forget to do X, Y, and Z later. Of course, trying not to think about something is impossible! You know the acid test for that, right? Try not to think about a pink elephant. There you have it. Pink elephants all around. This is what tends to happen when we try not to think about that task that comes to us in prayer. It just sits there and grows larger and larger like an overgrown pink elephant, effectively blocking out everything around it.

And then there was choice number two. I could hit *pause* on my prayer time and tend to the pressing thing. Best-case scenario, I would address the urgent matter and be able to return to prayer … but this was rare. Worst-case scenario—and the one that played out far more often—I would get distracted during my distraction by yet another distraction and not make it back to prayer at all.

I'm delighted to offer a third and better option for everyone who wants to learn how to enjoy God's company and like so many of my prayer habits, it's incredibly simple! But before I get to it, let's talk about simplicity.

My managing editor and I were on zoom recently discussing this project. Amy knew (because I may have already mentioned it a half dozen times during our meeting) how committed I was to writing with black and white clarity so believers can truly benefit from this book. She also knew that despite rudimentary teaching being my stated goal, I was nonetheless susceptible to feeling like my prayer habits are too basic, too elementary. (I may have been confessing that at every turn as well!) I was in the middle of one of these overthinking moments when Amy spoke words that brought rest to my second-guessing soul. I believe they'll help you embrace this chapter's prayer habit too.

"Remember, Shellie," Amy said. "Simple can be an effective strategy!" While that counsel was soaking in, Amy added a fitting analogy that sealed it for me. She didn't realize I was an ex-basketball coach when she said, "You know, a coach doesn't yell intricate information from the sideline during a heated competition. The coach delivers clear, concise instructions, and it's usually something the players already know but could use a reminder!" Boom! This ex-coach felt that.

TRYING NOT TO THINK ABOUT YOUR TO-DO LIST JUST MAKES IT LOOM LARGER. SO TAKE A NOTE!

So let me encourage you. The next time your brain starts coughing up all the things you need to do while you're trying to pray, stop and *take a note*. You'll find it frees your mind and allows you to continue!

The online dictionary I just searched defines the meaning behind the phrase *take a note* as "giving attention to something, especially because it is important." I like that. When I do stop and take a note, I'm acknowledging that while the matter is important enough to be addressed, it still doesn't get to usurp my time alone with God.

When I first began taking a note, I would reach for sticky pads or use the notes falling out of my Bible to jot down reminders. Then I started using the notepad on my phone. I've since discovered something that works even better for me. I grab my phone and shoot myself an email. You'll need to experiment and figure out what works best for you but do heed this warning: If you tend to get pulled into that device, stick with paper! For me, my early morning reminders are waiting for me whenever I do make it to my desk and start weeding through the inbox, and I don't have to worry about losing those mental notes or keeping up with the paper ones! Whatever you decide to use to catch those thoughts, I believe you'll discover that taking a note quiets the noise in your head and allows you to linger longer in God's transformative company.

However, taking a note is more than an effective defensive strategy for the to-dos that distract us in prayer. It's also an offensive move, and one that can actually strengthen our relationship with the Lord. I'll explain but first let's sit with a beautiful passage from God's Word that will help us build this final point. We're going to read a lengthy excerpt, but because God's Word is infinitely more helpful and faith-building for all of us than mine could ever be, let's pump the brakes and give our full attention to this familiar but profound passage from Psalm 139.

> *Lord, You have searched me and known me. You know when I sit down and when I get up; You understand my thought from far away. You scrutinize my path and my lying down, and are acquainted with all my ways. Even before there is a word on my tongue, behold, Lord, You know it all. You have encircled me behind and in front, and placed Your hand upon me. Such knowledge is too wonderful for me; it is too high, I cannot comprehend it. Where can I go from Your Spirit? Or where can I flee from Your presence? If I ascend to heaven, You are there; if I make my bed in Sheol, behold, You are there. If I take up the wings of the dawn, if I dwell in the remotest part of the sea, even there Your hand will lead me, and Your right hand will take hold of me. If I say, "Surely the darkness will overwhelm me, and the light around me will be night," even darkness is not dark to You, and the night is as bright as the day. Darkness and light are alike to You. For You created my innermost parts; You wove me in my mother's*

> *womb. I will give thanks to You, because I am awesomely and wonderfully made; wonderful are Your works, and my soul knows it very well. My frame was not hidden from You when I was made in secret, and skillfully formed in the depths of the earth; Your eyes have seen my formless substance; and in Your book were written all the days that were ordained for me, when as yet there was not one of them. How precious also are Your thoughts for me, God! How vast is the sum of them! Were I to count them, they would outnumber the sand. When I awake, I am still with You.* (Psalm 139:1–18)

Ahh. That is such a *selah* passage. *Selah* is a gorgeous Hebrew word that means "to pause" or "to lift up, exalt."[3] It invites us to take a deep breath and sit quietly with what we've just heard. The stirring words of this psalm remind us that nothing about our lives escapes God's notice, and it holds the key for us to have the confidence to stop and address our persistent to-dos without feeling like it's a sign of defeat.

Why? Because every time we stop to take a note with the goal of staying in God's presence, rather than allowing the endless details of our days to wreak havoc with our desire for Him, we essentially drive a stake in the ground. All of heaven witnesses our hunger for God winning out over the cares of this life. We're bowing to God's omnipotence, believing He knows everything that concerns us and trusting Him with it all.

TAKING A NOTE IS CHOOSING GOD'S PRESENCE OVER THE WORLD'S PRESSURE.

By taking a note and tending to it later, we're saying we believe the God who is waiting for us in the next moment knows what we need in this one. We're acknowledging His reign over every single

3. H5542. *selah*. *Strong's Hebrew Concordance*.

line item in our organizers and day planners and that's the kind of trust that will act like dry tinder to our heart's desire to know God. Try it and watch the Lover of your soul light the match.

Hugs,
Shellie

Pray with Me

Dear heavenly Father, these brains You gave us have an incredible ability to think about so many things all at once! And yet as grateful as we are for the potential our mental computers offer, they can also be quite frustrating when they whirl on and on and distract us from our goal of spending time with You. Thankfully, we know this mental activity comes as no surprise to You, our Creator, and that thought alone encourages us in our desire to pray! We look to You now to help us quiet the noise in our heads. There are so many thoughts that come to us that we don't need to remember, and then there are the other tasks and to-dos we don't need to forget! As we sit in prayer, give us discernment to know the difference and to trust that if we take a note, You'll give us time and wisdom to address those tasks later. We acknowledge our great need for Holy Spirit to help unite our minds and guard our hearts in prayer, and we're grateful that our heart's desire for Your company was born first in Yours. In the sweet name of Jesus, we pray. Amen.

Practice with Me

I'll give you three guesses about what our practice round is going to be today and the first two don't count. Oh, I knew you could do it. Now let's see you put all of that genius into action. During your next devotional time, use the lines below to write down any important to-dos that come to you so you can address them afterward. Or use your phone's notepad or email app if you prefer. Just beware of that great big vacuuming sound. Getting sucked in and sidetracked defeats the purpose.

PRAYER HABIT #6

DISCOVER THE POWER OF THE SPOKEN (PRAYER) WORD.

~HUGS, SHELLIE

6

LET HIM HEAR YOU NOW

Habit #6 – Discover the power of the spoken (prayer) word.

The Good Book sanctions both silent and audible prayer. It's not an either/or debate. I thought I'd put this right up front so no one feels the need to pick a side and choose their team colors. We're all tailgating at the same party, so keep your seat, friends. We'll look at some Scripture shortly to prove God hears both. Right now, I'd like to put a story on the table.

I remember a Sunday morning many years ago at my home church when the subject of whether it was okay to pray silently or if we should pray aloud came up during a classroom discussion. Out of respect for the friend in this story, I've chosen not to use her real name. Instead, I'm calling her Ruth, a good biblical name, in part because it's my beloved late grandmother's name, and I miss her so. But also because I should be safe in telling this since we don't have any Ruths in our ladies' group, and as far I can recall, we never have. I can't explain why I remember Ruth's words as clearly as I do when I can forget to stop and buy milk for days on end, but there you go. My husband is mystified by my wiring too.

Ruth began by saying she didn't think praying aloud was important. Many of those present agreed. And then she said the part that has so stayed with me. I think Ruth spoke for many of us when she confessed that if and when she managed to get a little time to herself, whether it was driving in the car or doing a routine household chore, she liked to just, "Take a break from everything and pray silently to myself."

Now I'm going to be stating the obvious here, but Ruth did not mean she was addressing her prayers to herself and trusting herself to answer them. And yet that's how I heard her words then and it's how I hear them replaying now, all these years later. Strange? Probably, but I'm hoping the phrasing of those words can help me explain why praying aloud has been such a significant help to me. Here's the sum of it: Opening my mouth and praying audibly has a way of shifting something in me and helping my prayer time feel more like a conversation with the Lord and less like I'm talking to myself. This despite the fact that praying aloud when I'm alone usually feels awkward, at least initially. And yet this very awkwardness begins to move me out of the way so I can pray. I realize that will need some explanation. Let me try to sharpen my point.

Every morning, I come to my prayer time with the same goals. I want to sit with God, worship Him, love on Him, and honor Him. I want to know more of Him than I did the day before. I come with yesterday's experience assuring me that prayer is more than just a worthy endeavor. God's company is worth every reach and every grasp.

And yet, more often than not, I'll find it ridiculously difficult, again, to still my thoughts and enter into prayer. I've spoken about this in earlier chapters, so you're probably getting used to my confessions. Perhaps they're beginning to make you wonder why you should even listen to me talk about prayer. That's fair, but if you'll stay with me, I promise my transparency has a purpose.

You and I have an enemy who works tirelessly to keep us out of God's transformative, soul-satisfying presence. None of us will ever arrive at a place where the devil's ugly voice won't insinuate that we're wasting our time and spinning our wheels in reaching for our Father. My goal in losing all pretense in these pages is to encourage you in this life-giving pursuit of God. I want to help you persevere in your desire to develop a prayer life because of the great reward I know awaits you—namely God Himself. Praying audibly is just one more strategy I've found helpful in connecting with the Father, and I'm convinced it can benefit you too. But why? Why does praying aloud help? Isn't that the question? I've already hinted at one answer when I said it begins to move me out of the way. Let's explore that.

> *My voice You shall hear in the morning, O Lord; in the morning I will direct it to You, and I will look up.*
>
> (Psalm 5:3 NKJV)

Those are sweet words. Almost every night, I whisper them to the Lord when I'm falling asleep, and I mean them. Until I don't. Which is usually the next morning when I'm feeling more like Ruth. Remember Ruth, my friend who admitted that when it came to praying aloud, she would rather not exert the energy, that she preferred to just sit quietly and pray to herself? That is me most mornings. I know my soul needs to pray but my *want to* is much slower to settle in and engage.

Do I have to pray aloud when that happens? Nope. But if I give in to my *want to* and sit in silence, I create space for my thoughts to begin circling and my eyelids to start growing heavy. Every single time this happens, I have a choice. I can tell my soul to shape up and speak out, or I can languish in hit-or-miss, halfhearted prayers until time gets away from me and I have to start the day bereft of the intimacy with God I crave.

God is always giving us choices like this.

He also gifts us with vocal cords and the breath that rushes over them to produce words. Were He to withdraw His breath, all life would cease. (See Job 34:14–15.) Like the great apostle Paul, my aim is to die daily so I can know Christ more dearly. It's why I see the choice of opening my mouth in prayer and lifting my voice as one more way to stick a fork in the eye of my selfish right to me and my enduring preference for what is easier and less demanding. In Mark 12:30 (NKJV), Jesus echoes a command from the Old Testament when He says, "*And you shall love the* Lord *your God with all your heart, with all your soul, with all your mind, and with all your strength.*" For me, praying aloud is one way to love the Lord with my strength because it takes *effort* I can often be reluctant to exert. However, the sweet reality of my experience is that acknowledging His supremacy over my inclinations invites His presence. This is what I meant by saying that audible praying helps to move me out of the way.

PRAYING ALOUD MAY TAKE EFFORT, BUT OH! THE SWEET REALITY OF INVITING HIS PRESENCE.

Here's something else I've discovered about praying audibly. When I pray in my head, I have a tendency to pray in monotone. But when I pray aloud, my heart gets involved with more feeling and emphasis. I don't necessarily understand why this is true and I'm not trying to teach this as doctrine. I'm simply sharing my experience. Praying aloud stirs me up and helps me stay present as I pray. Bonus? As of this writing, I've never fallen asleep while praying aloud, so there's that.

While everything I've just written is true of my experience, I don't always pray aloud, nor do I always keep praying audibly just because I start that way. Different situations call for different responses to the Father. For instance, sometimes after I've placed my obstinate want-to at His feet and pushed through audibly, I'll sense His invitation to, "*Be still, and know that I am God*" (Psalm 46:10 NKJV). Those moments are sacred pleasures, and silence is always the best and right response. There are other times when I'm too overwhelmed and the situation I find myself in is so dire, all I can offer up are tears and groans. Praise God, He hears that too, and He has provided for it.

> *Now in the same way the Spirit also helps our weakness; for we do not know what to pray for as we should, but the Spirit Himself intercedes for us with groanings too deep for words; and He who searches the hearts knows what the mind of the Spirit is, because He intercedes for the saints according to the will of God.* (Romans 8:26–27)

What a bleak and hopeless situation we'd all be in if God's hearing depended on our choosing the right words! We'll talk more about this shared experience shortly. Right now, I'm compelled to stop and lay the biblical foundation we spoke of earlier that supports both praying aloud and praying silently. I've already cited one of my favorite Scriptures about praying aloud. Remember? "*My voice You shall hear in the morning*" (Psalm 5:3 NKJV). That type of language is all over the Psalms.

> *My lips shall greatly rejoice when I sing to You, and my soul, which You have redeemed. My tongue also shall talk of Your righteousness all the day long.* (Psalm 71:23–24 NKJV)

> *I cry out to the LORD with my voice; with my voice to the LORD I make my supplication. I pour out my complaint before Him; I declare before Him my trouble.* (Psalm 142:1–2 NKJV)

Indeed, the Psalms are heavy with such recorded prayers, but audible praying isn't limited to that one book. God's people are shown lifting up their voices to Him all over the Bible. We can find men and women like Moses, Miriam, Deborah, Daniel, Peter, and Paul crying out to God, but our supreme example is Jesus Himself lifting His voice! What a treasure trove the prayers of Jesus are for us! Did God the Father know what God the Son was thinking? Absolutely, but Jesus still prayed aloud, and you can mark me down as beyond grateful. I'm specifically thinking of John 17 right now. We unpacked it in chapter 2. Remember? That tutorial has helped me learn to pray for others while being life-giving to me at the same time!

The Son of God's motivation for allowing Himself to be heard praying far exceeds my commentary about it but do consider the strength and encouragement generations of believers have found in His prayer words. Is this at least one of the reasons He lifted His voice to His Father in the hearing of His New Testament followers and why the Spirit made sure His words were recorded for us? You'd be hard-pressed to convince me otherwise.

I believe the benefit we experience hearing Jesus pray also speaks to the gift you and I extend to each other in corporate prayer. I've often witnessed the prayers of fellow saints change a room's atmosphere, reset a conversation, and encourage others to trust God and keep seeking Him, simply because of the words of faith they lifted publicly. And because we learn by example, praying aloud is also a valuable tool in the body of Christ to help fellow believers learn to pray.

YOUR AUDIBLE PRAYER CAN ENCOURAGE SOMEONE ELSE'S SILENT STRUGGLE.

While these are some of the reasons I encourage opening our mouths in prayer, I'll remind you of what I said earlier; this is not an either/or debate. We need both. Let's look at some of the biblical examples that support the blessing of God hearing silent prayer.

There's a story in the first book of Samuel about a woman named Hannah. Short backstory? She came to the temple to pray for God to open her womb. Month after month, she had dreamed of carrying a child. Time and again, her hopes had risen and crashed. The succinct record of her silent prayers are found along with the accusation of Eli, the residing priest, who surely added insult to her injury:

> *Hannah was praying in her heart, and her lips were moving but her voice was not heard. Eli thought she was drunk.*
> (1 Samuel 1:13 NIV)

Wow. We could have a conversation about church hurt here, but let's not. The topic inflicts enough misery and drains enough oxygen from the body of Christ without my speaking to it here. I'd rather celebrate what happened after Hannah's silent words were misunderstood by man. God saw, God heard, and it wasn't long before Hannah was craving pickles. By the way, that truth also holds healing balm for church wounds. God sees all. He is just and He can always be trusted, even when His people can't.

One more? How about Nehemiah? I love the guy and not just because he once got so frustrated with God's disobedient kids that he *"confronted them and cursed them and beat some of them and pulled out their hair"* (Nehemiah 13:25 ESV). To be clear, the Bible nowhere condones his actions and I'm not encouraging us to mimic him, but I will confess, there are times when I want to be righteously angry and pull a Neah-Maria myself. I don't, of course. All I have to do is consider the long-suffering love God has shown to me and I stand down faster than quick!

So here's Nehemiah's backstory: He was a Jew born in captivity and living in Persia during the Jewish exile. His day job was serving King Artaxerxes as an advisor and cupbearer. Being cupbearer was a big deal. It meant he tasted the king's food and drink before the king did to make sure no one was trying to poison him. Cupbearers were trusted and important, but perks aside, I'm not sure I would've wanted the job. One bad meal and it was lights out.

One day, Nehemiah was serving the king with his lip ran out so far, he could trip on it. That's southern speak for Nehemiah was visibly sad. Word had made it back to him that the city walls of his beloved Jerusalem were in disrepair and God's people were scattered and backslidden. Nehemiah's long face got the king's attention and prompted him to ask his cupbearer what was wrong.

Scripture records Nehemiah's response: "*Then I prayed to the God of heaven, and I answered the king*" (Nehemiah 2:4–5 NIV). Kudos, Nehemiah!

I have a word for that kind of short 911 prayer, the type I send up to the Lord while I'm having a real-time conversation with someone else and I need to know what to say, even while they're waiting on me to say it! I call it prayer peddling. Nehemiah told the king what was happening back home and why he was sad. The whole account is a fantastic read, but I want to point out what happened next. The king ended up sending Nehemiah to repair the walls with all the necessary authority, potential supplies, and financial assistance he could possibly need to accomplish the job! God responded to Nehemiah's silent prayer peddling with wisdom and provision as surely as He drew near to the saints who cried to Him aloud. And He will do the same for you and me.

The Bible is clear that our silent and audible prayers are acceptable, and they're all heard. If we are sensitive to Holy Spirit in prayer, we'll know which one fits the need of the moment. Be encouraged. The God of heaven and earth knows what we're going to say before we say it and He listens when we do. His Word says, "*Before they call, I will answer; while they are still speaking, I will listen*" (Isaiah 65:24)—and yet He still wants to hear from us. That's amazing. It's also motivating and humbling. Selah.

Hugs,
Shellie

Pray with Me

Dear heavenly Father, I want to remember that my voice is a gift from You, and it's a privilege to return it to You. Remind me that there is no one way to communicate with You that excludes another. Instead, help me to be sensitive in prayer to the need of the moment and the situation. Will You show me the motives of my heart? Alert me when I'm praying silently because I'm tired or sleepy and I'm giving in to my broken *want-to*. I confess that I'm often lazy in prayer. Forgive me and make me new. I want my words and my attitude to be acceptable in Your sight, my Rock and my Redeemer. In the sweet name of Jesus, I pray. Amen.

Practice with Me

One way to practice audible praying is by breathing out little snippets of prayer throughout the day. The opportunities will be as endless as God is infinite! Stepping in a big old bubble bath? Whisper words of gratitude for the warm water (or piping hot if you're like me!) that feels so good to your skin and bones. You can also take a moment to pray for those who don't have access to clean water. Is it a gorgeous sunny day? Audibly thank the Lord for the beauty of it. Rainy day? Give thanks aloud for what the rain is doing to replenish the ground. I'm sure you're getting the idea, but here are a couple more. If you're walking into work or punching that clock on your way out the door, you can open your mouth and say, "Lord, thank You for this job that helps me provide for my family." You don't like your job? Even while you're giving thanks for the job you do have, you can ask the Lord to open doors for another one. It may be in His will to move you. The point is that using our voice to speak to the Lord throughout the day begins to build in us a familiarity with audible praying that replaces our initial awkwardness and seeps into our dedicated prayer times. Ask me how I know! Bonus? We soon discover we're praying without ceasing! And who would've ever believed we could do that? God. God did. Praise Him! Jot down some things that inspired you to pray aloud today.

PRAYER HABIT #7

NATURE MAKES A GREAT PRAYER PARTNER.

~HUGS, SHELLIE

7

THIS IS OUR FATHER'S WORLD

Habit #7 – Nature makes a great prayer partner.

As I sit here writing to you from my back porch, the sun is beginning to sink over the lake in my backyard in what has been a startling beautiful, crystal-clear Louisiana day. Squirrels are chasing each other up, down, and around our big old oak tree. A couple of egrets are croaking as they stalk the lake bank. "Argh!" is my best imitation of the big white birds' repetitive communication. I hope they're happier than they seem because they sound like exasperated pirates.

The occasional fish breaks the surface of the water and disappears in a splash, and I hear more bird calls than I can identify. Hank, our white Labrador Retriever, is hanging close. He's hoping to convince me to call it quits and play, but I've got too many words left in me this evening. I want to talk to you about our Father's world and how He designed it to speak to us.

In my peripheral vision is the porch sign featuring one of my favorite quotes, and not just because the body of water in front of me is named Lake Providence, though I admit that might have been one of the reasons I first bought it. But all these years later, I don't have to turn my head for the words to echo inside me. They were spoken a hundred years ago by Mary Webb, late English writer and poet, but her words call to me like she's sitting right here, reminding me that, "*The well of Providence is deep. It's the buckets we bring to it that are small.*" Amen, Mary. I'm aiming to remember.

My husband Phil, aka the beloved farmer, hung some round, solar-powered lights in the thick gnarly branches of the old oak tree last year. They're beginning to glow as the pinks and light blues of the sky deepen into violet, navy, and shades of gold while I keep pecking out words, deleting them, and auditioning more. How can I hope to explain the benefits of spending time listening for God in nature when poets and preachers much more learned and eloquent than I have written so much on the subject? I'm admittedly daunted by the challenge, but I'm willing to take my turn at it.

Perhaps there's no better place to begin than with Psalm 19. It holds serious motivation for enlisting nature to help us learn to pray. I memorized the words of this chapter years ago in the King James translation. (And I still love King Jimmy!) But I especially like the way the Amplified Version handles the last few lines of verses 1–4.

> *The heavens are telling of the glory of God; and the expanse [of heaven] is declaring the work of His hands. Day after day pours forth speech, and night after night reveals knowledge. There is no speech, nor are there [spoken] words [from the stars]; their voice is not heard. Yet their voice [in quiet evidence] has gone out through all the earth, their words to the end of the world.* (Psalm 19:1–4 AMP)

The psalmist tells us nature speaks. Trees are described as clapping their hands in Isaiah 55:12 and lifting their voices to sing in 1 Chronicles 16:33. I believe those who choose to lean in and listen can learn to hear all of creation calling out to the Creator. Even better, we can join the conversation for our good and God's glory. Let me explain by showing you what this looks like for me.

When weather permits, I love nothing more than slipping down to the dock for early morning prayer and positioning myself to listen. Some of the sweetest moments of my life with God have been spent on that dock. But just in case anyone is picturing me as Cinderella with the birds twittering merrily around me and squirrels performing circus tricks for my entertainment, allow me to pause for a reality reset. By way of reminder, I live in northeast Louisiana. I'm far more likely to be swatting mosquitoes large enough to carry off my coffee cup, fanning an endless assault of gnats, or worse. And now, I'm going to need to illustrate *or worse* because I jumped a story with those last words. Jumping a story is like a hunter surprising a rabbit, only nothing will get shot. I could try not to tell it, but I'll be distracted until I do. Oh, and I'll acknowledge up front that it doesn't hold great teaching potential but as I'm fond of pointing out, "Life is better when you're laughing."

HAVING NATURE AS A PRAYER PARTNER CAN BRING YOU MANY SURPRISES.

It happened early one morning while I was praying down on the dock. I had scalding hot coffee in one hand and my smartphone in the other. I believe I had opened my camera app to try and capture a picture of an egret, or a turtle … or maybe a cloud. The world will never know. The moment blew up and I have been unsuccessful at recalling those pre-hissy fit details.

My first hint of trouble was a little tickly feeling around my chin. I assumed it was a strand of hair and smoothed it away. (I'm shuddering here.) Moments later, I felt something similar on my neck, and it was moving. Oh, surely not. May I remind you my hands were full of hot coffee and a phone that does not know how to swim and didn't need to get thrown into the lake. (Spoiler alert, it didn't get dunked, but don't get lost on the details. It very well could have been!)

With the pinky finger of my shaking hand that was also holding said smartphone, I pulled the collar of my pajama top out and looked down. Yes, ma'am. Yes, sir. There it was. A big hairy spider … on my stomach. I'll pause while you consider that development.

Are we good? There was a spider perched on my person, and I promise you, the thing was staring me down. I'm talking eye contact! It wasn't just any spider either. It was a Louisiana dock spider. Think baby tarantula.

Now, there have been some people, among them the beloved farmer, who suggested that I should have smushed the intruder against my belly. I know, right?! I don't understand some people.

For five hundred and seventy-five years, or two to three seconds, I tried shaking that spider out of my business, but he ran around under my pj's successfully avoiding my efforts and ignoring my screams. Can spiders hear? If so, his feelings were hurt because I was calling down curses from heaven on his furry self the entire time.

Somehow, in the middle of the mania—and I need props for this—I managed to teleport myself to the house and inside the back door before I removed my clothes. I am the first to admit the beloved farmer has to put up with a lot of shenanigans and probable embarrassment from me being *in the public eye,* so to speak. That said, I would like the record to reflect that I did not put the public's eye out by getting nekkid on the dock. Although I thought about it.

As that unfortunate story illustrates, my morning prayer sessions aren't all filled with the whisper of angel wings and quiet meditative moments. Just like the rest of my life, and yours, my dock devotions are most often filled with real-world challenges. But oh, it's worth it! There are many benefits to communing with God outdoors. Let's look at a few of them together.

We'll begin with the most practical application I can give you. Praying outside helps me forget about the responsibilities waiting for me inside. I can't see my desk, hear the clothes dryer, or wonder at the layer of dust on my furniture. Is it just me or is dusting a total waste of time and energy? Someone once said, "The Bible says we come from dust, and we return to dust, so she doesn't dust just in case it's someone she once knew." Sounds like a plan I could sign on to but please don't tell my mother I said that. The Queen of Us All once vacuumed her attic. I'm not joking.

For those of you who are always on top of everything in your house and systematically checking things off of your well-planned schedule (I tried to type that with a straight face!), here's another benefit to praying outdoors. Creation reminds us of how big and powerful our God is and how small and dependent we are. James 4:14 describes our lives as vapors. It can be hard to feel the weight of those words when we're surrounded by the bells and whistles of technology and man-made materials. There's often a buffer of sorts between that truth and our experience when we're indoors. But when we sit exposed to the awe of this complex and teeming world around us and consider that God spoke it all into being and it will keep turning long after we're gone, we learn humility—and the practice of humility invites God's presence. *"Draw near to God and He will draw near to you"* (James 4:8 NKJV). I've found I have to be intentional about giving myself regular opportunities to experience this powerful prayer habit from nature.

Regardless of whether I'm traveling and taking in brand new vistas or sitting on my own dock in our small hometown, the universe always extends beyond my field of vision and carries on independent of my existence. Should I walk out of the scene, nothing changes. Should God withdraw His breath, everything would perish, myself included. (See Psalm 104:29.) Sitting quietly in nature is a humbling reminder of how much I need God. It encourages worship and gives weight to my prayers.

CREATION SPEAKS VOLUMES WHEN I QUIET MYSELF TO LISTEN.

But ... about that talkative universe we read about in Psalm 19. Nature speaks, and she is a fine teacher. The late George Washington Carver, one of history's most famous botanists, gifted the world with a massive amount of helpful inventions, produced from a lifetime of listening for God while he studied the natural world around him, and the treasure of his quotes continue to inspire us. In one of my personal favorites, the lifelong learner spoke of nature as one of the ways God communicates with us:

> I love to think of nature as unlimited broadcasting stations, through which God speaks to us every day, every hour and every moment of our lives, if we will only tune in and remain so.[4]

Amen, Brother Carver! His words remind me of this encouragement from the Scriptures:

> *But ask the animals, and they will teach you, or the birds in the sky, and they will tell you; or speak to the earth, and it will teach you, or let the fish in the sea inform you. Which of all these does not know that the hand of the* Lord *has done this? In his hand is the life of every creature and the breath of all mankind.* (Job 12:7–10 NIV)

My testimony to you is that I rarely sit in nature without the Lord offering a lesson through something happening around me. Once, I was sitting on my back porch praying for someone I love dearly. She was in a dire situation. Her future seemed bleak, her situation complicated and irreparable. Although I had my head

4. Gary R. Kremer, ed., *George Washington Carver in His Own Words* (Columbia, MO: University of Missouri Press, 1987), 143.

bowed in prayer, the truth is I felt like my prayers were all falling to the ground. Doubts assailed me that morning. I wondered if I was even being heard, and then I felt shame for wondering again. Anybody else been there? Let me equip you with a succinct truth you can use the next time it happens: Faith shaming doesn't come from our Father. Refuse to give it a home in you.

Suddenly I felt impressed to raise my head and open my eyes. I obeyed and discovered a hummingbird hovering directly in front of me, mere inches from my face. Never before had a hummingbird found its way to my screened-in porch. (And it has never happened again.) I may have quit breathing for a second. It wasn't the details of the tiny bird's iridescent wings that moved me to awe, as exquisite as they were. The moment was deeper and sweeter than that. See, as long as I can remember, the loved one I was so concerned about that morning has been extremely fond of hummingbirds. She feeds the real ones and collects all kinds of man-made replicas. I felt my flighty guest reminding me that God knew every detail of the situation and my prayers were being heard. As quickly as he came, the little messenger was gone, but praise God, he left me with a renewed hope to energize my prayers. (And because I know you're wondering, He is still writing my loved one's story.)

I could tell you story after story of God speaking to me through creation. Some dramatic, like the hope of a hummingbird, others a bit more humorous. A while back, I met a fussy red robin who visited my backyard with a challenge for anyone with ears to hear. We'll call her Jill. She was hunting worms with her mate or her friend that morning. I admit my robin identification skills could use some sharpening, but since calling the pair Jack and Jill will help me tell the story, we'll stick with the nursery rhyme names. I'll set the scene for you.

I was praying on my porch when I noticed the two of them hopping into my line of vision, stage left. They were in a flower bed of evergreen liriope that is layered in pine straw. Jack was leading the way, but Jill was trailing right behind him, and forgive me, bird lovers, but she was pestering the tail feathers off her friend.

I watched the same scene playing out over and over, as if stuck on repeat. Jack would dig in the straw, come up without a worm, shake his head, take a hop or two, and dig again. And what was Jill doing? Was she helping? No, not even a little. Jill was staying one hop behind Jack, and every time he dug and came up empty-handed, she would squawk at him, as if to say, "Got a worm? Got a worm?" They must've repeated this process a dozen times before Jack flew off with Jill in hot pursuit. I can't say for sure that Jill was getting on Jack's last nerve, although she would've been jumping up and down on mine, but I can tell you what came to me as I watched them.

They reminded me of two believers, one fully determined to dig into God's Word for nourishment and another perfectly willing to let the other one do all the studying and live on the leftovers. "Got a word? Got a word?" I felt the weight of a tragedy that plays out all too often: God's desire to speak to each of us juxtaposed against those who won't take the time or make the effort to look and listen. You can decide whether the Lord was talking to me through that scene or if I just have a healthy imagination. I won't be offended if you go with the second option. I wondered, too, at least that first day. But the same scene played out before me the very next morning with two birds who looked identical to the first pair and performed their act on the same stage, aka flower bed. Isn't that just a little curious?

Friend, our imaginations are a gift from God, as surely as our physical senses. This means they can be profitable for our spiritual instruction and fuel for our growth. But hear me, this truth applies only as far as our imaginations are submitted to Him. Thoughts that aren't submitted to God can quickly become vain imaginations that wreak havoc in our lives. (See 2 Corinthians 10:5.) Here's a surefire litmus test: If our imaginations are being used to puff up self or promote man, flee from them! A sanctified imagination will always lead us to glorify God and the further enjoyment of Him.

The message I took from the robins made me want to watch for Him and listen for Him all the more. I knew I was safe to learn from it because it lined up with the revelation of Scripture. Through His cross, burial, and resurrection, Jesus reconciled sinful man with holy God. He made a way for each of us who believe to know God personally and to hear from Him individually. God desires this communion with us more than we could ever desire to commune with Him. Takeaway? Don't be like Jill. Be like Jack.

Hugs,

Shellie

Pray with Me

Dear heavenly Father, thank You for being willing to talk to me through nature, for using Your creation as one more tool to teach me. I want to practice listening and hearing from You! Help me yield my eyes and ears to You for Your purposes. Protect me from vain imaginations as I listen for You! Do not let me be deceived as I seek You. I want to make good use of every mental faculty You've given me, and that includes my imagination, but remind me to always test my thoughts and conclusions against Your written Word. I praise You for the treasure of Your Word, for I know You will never contradict Yourself. The litmus test of Your written Word gives me peace. I commit my ways to You, to follow Your peace and not my own understanding. In Jesus's sweet name, I pray. Amen.

Practice with Me

While the material we've covered in this chapter is fresh on your mind, look for the first available opportunity to practice what we've discussed. Find a place to sit outside. And please don't feel like it has to be a glorious beach scene with crashing waves or a beautiful mountain path like you might expect to see on your social feeds. Simply find a place to sit with the Lord. Now, watch what is happening around you and listen for God's still small voice in your heart. Record anything you believe you heard below. Does a passage of Scripture come to mind? Look it up. If you're a new believer or one who doesn't have a lot of God's Word hidden in your heart, at least not yet (smile), here's a simple help: type key words from your time listening into your favorite search engine along with the words "Bible" or "Scripture." Your search might look like this: "Bible verses about the clouds." Read and record any verses you want to remember. Congrats! You're building a treasure trove God can use to speak to you in the days ahead!

PRAYER HABIT #8

SAY NO TO PRAYER QUOTAS.

~HUGS, SHELLIE

8

WHEN LOSING COUNT IS A GOOD THING

Habit #8 – Say no to prayer quotas.

My name is Shellie, and I count things. I count and measure anything and everything. The world may never know how many licks it takes to get to the center of a Tootsie Roll Pop, but it won't be because your friend here hasn't tried to count them. Nor can I tell you how many strokes of a kayak paddle it takes to get from my dock to the end of the lake, or how many coats of mascara I apply during my extreme makeovers every morning, mainly because something else gets my attention before I can finish tallying, but interruptions never dissuade me from trying. In addition to counting, I compete continuously—with myself! I'm always trying to beat yesterday's numbers or given expectations. Should the app on my phone say it will take an hour and six minutes to get to my destination, I want to arrive in an hour five!

If you were diagnosing me as you read and preparing to send helpful medical links, I appreciate it, but please don't go to any trouble on my account. I say that with genuine kindness. I've done the research, and while it's true that counting can signal an obsessive-compulsive disorder, apparently casual counting can also be normal behavior that doesn't warrant concern. There are ways to determine if you're just a happy counter by nature, like me, or if you're truly suffering from arithmomania (obsessive counting) and you need intervention. The legal eagles on my team would like me to note that I'm not a doctor and I've never even played one on TV, so this shouldn't be taken as dependable medical advice. Okay, but here's the general idea.

If you can't control your desire to count, if losing count causes you anxiety, if you feel you can't move on to the next task unless you finish counting, or if your counting is having a negative impact on your daily activities, you might want to consult a professional. I can honestly say none of those issues apply to me. I never get anxious about counting. Nor do I feel compelled to finish a count and I can lose my place as quickly as I begin without batting an eye. I guess I'm normal, at least where counting is concerned. So why bring it up? Because there is one area where counting and measuring will prove to be our Achilles' heel, every single time, and you can count on it. (Some puns write themselves.)

When it comes to our desire to learn how to enjoy God's company in prayer, counting and measuring are our archenemies. That's my loads of experience speaking. I've chronicled much of my faith walk in my earlier books like *Heart Wide Open*[5] and *Finding Deep and Wide*. We won't re-plow all that ground here, but I will need to recap it to set up the meat of this chapter.

In short, I'm recovering from the bondage of performance religion. Please note I avoided using the word *recovered*. That's because I'm determined to own my present-tense vulnerability to that trap. I know it's only fixing my eyes on Jesus that keeps me free of it. Here's a bit more of the story.

I came to faith early in life. It's hard to remember when I didn't believe in God and trust in the finished work of Jesus, His Son. And yet for many years, I lived with Jesus *on the side*, so to speak.

---

5. Shellie Rushing Tomlinson, *Heart Wide Open: Trading Mundane Faith for an Exuberant Life with Jesus* (New York: WaterBrook Press, 2014).

I felt like we were good, after all. He had paid and I had prayed. End of story. I had little desire to know more of Him. All I really wanted was to do my own thing, provided I had enough eternal security mixed in to feel good about judgment day. Thankfully, any assurance of my salvation was elusive. God never let me find rest for my soul while I was living for me and I'm forever grateful because it led me to truth. Jesus *is* life and outside of Him, there is only endless searching.

Fast forward a bit. Once I finally became Jesus hungry, I wanted all of Him I could get. Again, I covered the how and why of that life change in my previous books. Suffice for this discussion, I fell smack into the trap of performance religion. Instead of feasting on Jesus, living in His light, and letting Him transform me, I was always connecting my assessment of how well I was doing or not doing with how welcome I was to enjoy His presence. Mark this next thought down where you can see it over and again: *We don't mature or produce fruit to get into God's presence; His presence matures us and produces fruit in our lives.* I repeat:

GOD'S PRESENCE MATURES US AND PRODUCES FRUIT IN OUR LIVES.

You've probably heard it said, "If you don't measure it, you can't improve it." There is wisdom in those words and appropriate times to apply them. We'll address the benefits before we're done with this chapter, but for someone who loves to set goals and reach them, who values checklists and achievements, measuring can easily become spiritual quicksand. I've often rued those days when I was always trying to *buckle down so I could measure up* enough to enjoy His company. It's an exhausting way to live, and it is not the inheritance Jesus died to give us!

You may be wondering what all this counting and measuring talk has to do with this chapter's prayer habit. I haven't forgotten. We're just now ready to address it.

Although I run from legalism now because I've seen how ugly it is, I live acknowledging that I can still fall into that trap. And nowhere is this more obvious to me than when I set out to spend time with God in prayer. I'm fully convinced of the futility of evaluating my walk to earn my welcome, but my praying self can succumb to amnesia about measuring and counting faster than I can say, "Dear Lord." Just that quickly, I can get all tangled up again in my get 'er done, count and measure nature. I'll find myself acting like I need to hit some hidden prayer quota, as if my time spent with God has a minimum requirement and a maximum target or it doesn't qualify. Ugh.

Jesus addressed performance prayers in Matthew 6:5–8 when He said:

> *When you pray, you are not to be like the hypocrites; for they love to stand and pray in the synagogues and on the street corners so that they will be seen by people. Truly I say to you, they have their reward in full. But as for you, when you pray, go into your inner room, close your door, and pray to your Father who is in secret; and your Father who sees what is done in secret will reward you. And when you are praying, do not use thoughtless repetition as the Gentiles do, for they think that they will be heard because of their many words. So do not be like them; for your Father knows what you need before you ask Him.*

Confusing the act of performing our prayers with talking to our Father is a recipe for failure, whether we're offering our words publicly or privately.

With Holy Spirit's help, we can learn the better way. Over and over again, I find it necessary and good to remember that I'm in His presence to be with Him and enjoy Him, to learn of Him and from Him. I'm not there to earn His approval with my ability to stay on topic and pray without ceasing. (Oh, hallelujah!) That's not just the best news ever for me. It's God-glorifying, soul-satisfying, world-changing truth for the people He places on my heart in prayer. When I lay my tape measure and agenda before His throne, He can fill my empty hands with heavenly gifts for others.

Mind you, I never consciously try to count, measure, or perform my prayers. It's more of a trap I've learned I need to watch for and avoid. Left to myself, I'll slide back into the muddy pit more often than not. But praise God, none of His children are left to themselves! We have Holy Spirit!

Jesus said, *"I will ask the Father, and He will give you another Helper, so that He may be with you forever"* (John 14:16). That Helper is Holy Spirit, and He is ever present and faithful to teach us.

> *But the Helper, the Holy Spirit whom the Father will send in My name, He will teach you all things, and remind you of all that I said to you.* (John 14:26)

Included in Holy Spirit's transformative teaching is how and what to measure and when to lose count. You may be thinking, "How and what to measure?! Wait just a minute." After all my warnings about performance goals, that may have caught you by surprise. Hear me out. Not all evaluations are harmful. When handled biblically, examinations lead to deeper intimacy.

Counting and measuring is dangerous when we're relying on our positive tallies to feel like we can approach God in prayer or we're hesitant to approach Him because we've *checked the books* and concluded He is surely less than pleased with our efforts. That kind of quantifying is performance religion. It means we're trusting our works and not God's grace. That's altogether different from the healthy biblical habit of examining ourselves in the light of the Word. Remember when I said there was wisdom in the adage, "If you don't measure it, you can't improve it"? Let's circle back and pick up that thread.

As we've already noted, grace can't be purchased with works, and we can't chart enough progress to earn it. However, God's Word does direct us, repeatedly, to examine both our faith and our fruit. Here's the difference and it is life-changing: These assessments aren't done to earn the relationship freely given to us in Christ, but to check for signs that we *are* in Him and to make sure we're growing more like Him!

This type of evaluation is supported by Scripture.

> *Examine yourselves as to whether you are in the faith. Test yourselves. Do you not know yourselves, that Jesus Christ is in you?—unless indeed you are disqualified.*
> (2 Corinthians 13:5 NKJV)

> *For if anyone thinks himself to be something, when he is nothing, he deceives himself. But let each one examine his own work, and then he will have rejoicing in himself alone, and not in another.* (Galatians 6:3–4 NKJV)

> *Let's examine and search out our ways, and let's return to the* LORD. (Lamentations 3:40)

That said, Scripture never sets up prayer quotas. Allowing our daily devotions to become another goal-oriented activity is a pit waiting to swallow up all who long for God's company.

Catherine McAuley, founder of the Sisters of Mercy, once said, "Many a precious prayer has been said in a second." It's always a heart matter with the Lord, and He makes it clear that we need Holy Spirit's help to understand what's really going on in our ours.

> *Who can understand his errors? Cleanse me from secret faults.* (Psalm 19:12 NKJV)

> *Search me, O God, and know my heart; try me, and know my anxieties; and see if there is any wicked way in me, and lead me in the way everlasting.* (Psalm 139:23–24 NKJV)

Our spiritual checkups are prone to error when we conduct them in our own hearts with our own biases. The goal isn't to measure ourselves against ourselves, but to examine our lives in the light of God's Word. Without Holy Spirit, we'll put our fingers on the scale and the results will be inaccurate.

> *For we dare not class ourselves or compare ourselves with those who commend themselves. But they, measuring themselves by themselves, and comparing themselves among themselves, are not wise.* (2 Corinthians 10:12 NKJV)

> *Because you say, "I am rich, have become wealthy, and have need of nothing"—and do not know that you are wretched, miserable, poor, blind, and naked—I counsel you to buy from Me gold refined in the fire, that you may be rich; and white garments, that you may be clothed, that the shame of your nakedness may not be revealed; and anoint your eyes with eye salve, that you may see. As many as I love, I rebuke and chasten. Therefore, be zealous and repent.*
> (Revelation 3:17–19 NKJV)

Speaking of healthy counting, we haven't even talked about counting our blessings, which is always a boon to our prayer lives. We'll go there in the next chapter. I tend to believe prayers of gratitude and thanksgiving must be some of the sweetest we ever bring to Father's ears. For now, I'll recap and wrap with this: There are serious dangers to counting and evaluating, and there are great benefits. Thankfully, we have Holy Spirit to help us discern the difference. Let's live listening to Him!

Hugs,
Shellie

Pray with Me

Dear Lord, I've spent several thousand words in this chapter alone talking about the dangers of evaluating, and I find myself wondering if I handled this subject well or if I should erase it all and take another stab at it. That's almost comical. Almost. I wonder how it is that You bear with me, even as I remind myself that I stand in the favor You have for Your Son, my Savior. So I will glory at the mystery of the cross instead. Thank You, Jesus, for the price You paid to take our sin and clothe us in Your righteousness. Thank You for trading Your all-sufficiency for our inadequacies. We love You. We praise You, and we ask You to alert us when we're counting and measuring to gain what's ours. Teach us instead to come before You with grateful hearts, to submit to regular checkups from You, our Great Physician, and examine ourselves in the light of Your Word, all that we might grow more and more like You. Jesus, it's in Your sweet name we pray. Amen.

Practice with Me

Let's find time today to sit with God today and enjoy Him, without regard to how long we're there. We're going to surrender our prayer quotas and our tendency to try to make good-sounding prayers and aim to talk to Him from an open heart. While we're at it, let's fire ourselves from the job of trying to remember everything we *should* be praying for and trust Him to prompt our prayers as we enjoy His company. Let's breathe in and breathe out with Him, listening for Him. And let's do it again tomorrow. Jot down any prayer prompts God has given you today:

PRAYER HABIT #9

EXPERIENCE MORE OF THE GOD YOU CAN'T SEE BY ACKNOWLEDGING HIS BLESSINGS YOU CAN SEE.

~HUGS, SHELLIE

9

THE POWER OF THANK-YOU NOTES

Habit #9 – Experience more of the God you can't see by acknowledging His blessings you can see.

If you were raised by a Southern mama as I was, there's a solid chance that emboldened chapter title left you squirming a little or a lot, depending on where you are with your acknowledgments. I get you. Current situation? I just this minute ordered monogrammed thank-you notes because I've been out of them for a while, and I couldn't even think about penning this chapter until I tended to that oversight. (I'm looking at you, Mama.)

Our mother drilled my sisters and me on the importance of thank-you notes. Type in "thank you note" on my website, and you'll find photographic evidence of Mama practicing what she preaches in a blog post. Several years ago, I documented images from a proper handwritten thank-you note she had sent me, her own daughter, after one of her back surgeries. Bless her. Hadn't she already thanked me in person for the food, the care, and the company? Absolutely—several times over. But for Mama, the note sealed her sincerity.

Though many Southern mamas insist on their children writing thank-you notes from an early age for occasions like birthdays and Christmas, my sisters and I were actually allowed some leeway until our high school graduations and the arrival of those congratulatory gifts. Just like that, all pardons were over, and a new rule was put in place. Gift in, note out—asap. When I married the love of my life only a few short months after graduation (true story and a good one, but we'll need to save it), Mama doubled down on this social nicety. She called me daily with what I'm sure she thought were subtle inquiries on my thank-you note progress, but her investigation was about as inconspicuous as a SWAT team descending on a drug bust. In the South, the speed and content of thank-you notes reflects on the bride and groom's families, hence the group investment. I made my list, and Mama checked it twice, but my heart definitely wasn't in it.

I begin with these memories because I've discovered a powerful connection between acknowledging our blessings and experiencing God's company. It's been a great boon to my own prayer life, but if you're going to profit from this chapter, I need you to hear what I'm about to share as a *get-to* secret opportunity and not a *should-do* obligation. See, Mama's lesson eventually took and over time, writing thank-you notes has become important to me as well. Only these days, the notes I send are sincere ones. I hope they bless the intended party, but I've noticed something interesting. Because they come from the heart, I am blessed as I write them! Let me show you how this principle applies to our prayer lives.

This particular habit is hard to trace. It's been a while since I first began practicing it, and I can't tie it to a day when I had any discernible epiphany, but I'm convinced God planted the idea in my heart as a response to my repeated requests for Him to teach me what to do on the days when I come to prayer and—surprise!—the heavens feel like brass and God feels far away... again. I wrote that in present tense because it still happens.

I've truly grown to love prayer and yet those days when the veil between heaven and earth feels impenetrable come all the same. One may come tomorrow. If it does...

Granted, it may take me longer to remember to turn to this prayer habit than I would like, but once my remedial self recognizes the familiar challenge has returned, I'll begin thanking God for the very present-tense blessings of the moment. It may sound like, "Thank You, Lord, that I was able to get out of bed unassisted." From there, I might say, "Thank You, Lord, for the strength to begin this day" or "Thank You for the running water in the bathroom and the bite of food I'm enjoying from the pantry or refrigerator."

WHEN THE ONE MY SOUL LOVES FEELS DISTANT, I START BUILDING A MOUNTAIN OF GRATITUDE, ONE ACKNOWLEDGMENT AT A TIME.

I might continue with, "Thank You for the hot coffee in my hands and the fireplace warming my bones." Or if the weather is nice and I'm praying on the dock with Hank the Tank, I may thank God for making dogs with their endless capacity for devotion. Day by day, my oversized white Lab and reliably neurotic guard dog successfully chases dangerous fishermen away from our dock before they have a chance to pull off their intended assault. That's Hank's story anyway. The fishermen would say they were trolling by and hadn't planned to stop. You decide who you'll believe. But back to my point: the goal is to notice every good gift around me and begin acknowledging God for all the sights I'm seeing, the sounds I'm hearing, the unending lessons His creation is offering, and the miracle of another day on His planet. This practice has proven to be invaluable in stirring my heart to reach for God. When the One my souls loves feels distant, I simply ignore my feelings and start building a mountain of gratitude, one acknowledgement at a time, because I've discovered the power of living thanksgiving. When I start thanking the Lord for the things I can see, taste, and touch, the One I can't see begins to feel nearer still.

I have a working theory on why this is. Want to hear it?

We know God is inside and outside of time, right? We know He is before time, and He is beyond time. God exists in the past even as He is with us in the present and while He awaits us in the future. We also know such space-hopping time travel isn't our human experience. You and I, while destined for an eternity with this supernatural God, are currently bound by time's constraints. We can't reach into the past to connect with Him or into the future to be with Him. For us, the only moment holding out the opportunity to be with God is this one. And this one. And now, this one.

These marvelous mundane moments to experience His nearness are presented to us in the middle of mind-numbing normal routines that fill up our days, but they carry with them God's staggering and open-ended invitation to do life with Him. We want to say yes to God, yes to living in His presence, and yes to a nourishing prayer life that connects us to Him, but we struggle with the how-to. What if intentionally acknowledging His inimitable blessings is one way to foster this deeper connection we are craving? I would argue from experience that it is.

Many of the blessings I spoke of giving thanks for fall into a category theologians call *common grace*. The term describes the kindnesses of God poured out on both believers and unbelievers indiscriminately, like the sun warming our backs and the spring rain watering our fields, the enjoyment of friends and family, and the excitement born of travel and adventure. John Wesley, founder of the Methodist church, spoke of common grace as God's porch, where God's universal goodness and the beauty of our world draws man to His doorstep and encourages him to repent. I'm a porch girl, so that language speaks to me, but I think it can also help to explain why acknowledging these blessings can jump-start our prayers. Hold that thought while we ground this discussion in the following verses that underscore God's omnipotence and our dependence on Him.

> *Before the mountains were brought forth, or ever You had formed the earth and the world, even from everlasting to everlasting, You are God.* (Psalm 90:2 NKJV)

> *"I am the Alpha and the Omega," says the Lord God, "who is and who was and who is to come, the Almighty."* (Revelation 1:8)

> *Surely God will never do wickedly, nor will the Almighty pervert justice. Who gave Him charge over the earth? Or who appointed Him over the whole world? If He should set His heart on it, if He should gather to Himself His Spirit and His breath, all flesh would perish together, and man would return to dust.* (Job 34:12–15 NKJV)

> *Every good gift and every perfect gift is from above, coming down from the Father of lights, with whom there is no variation or shadow due to change.* (James 1:17 ESV)

All of those verses celebrate God's omnipotence and it's in our best interest to mediate on His otherness. It's good to sit with the truth that no man could ever replicate or manufacture the food, water, and light necessary to sustain life and consider that God could withdraw these basic building blocks at will, should He choose. It not only reminds us that all of life on planet Earth is by God's grace, it also becomes a valuable habit in prayer. Ask Job.

You remember Job, right? He was the Old Testament saint who had it all and lost it all. But it was the slice of humble pie served up by God Himself that changed the way Job saw everything. Some of my favorite lines of Scripture are in Job 38–39, where God begins to draw a distinction between Himself and, well, everyone else.

> *Then the* L*ORD* *answered Job from the whirlwind and said, "Who is this who darkens the divine plan by words without knowledge? Now tighten the belt on your waist like a man, and I shall ask you, and you inform Me! Where were you when I laid the foundation of the earth? Tell Me, if you have understanding, who set its measurements? Since you know. Or who stretched the measuring line over it? On what were its bases sunk? Or who laid its cornerstone, when the morning stars sang together and all the sons of God shouted for joy? Or who enclosed the sea with doors when it went out from the womb, bursting forth; when I made a cloud its garment, and thick darkness its swaddling bands, and I placed boundaries on it and set a bolt and doors, and I said, 'As far as this point you shall come, but no farther; and here your proud waves shall stop'? Have you ever in your life commanded the morning, and made the dawn know its place."* (Job 38:1–12)

God continues this vein of questioning for several chapters, and when He finally pauses, Job has had an outlook overhaul and learned a powerful lesson in humility. Let's listen to Job's response.

> *I know that You can do all things, and that no plan is impossible for You. "Who is this who conceals advice without knowledge?" Therefore I have declared that which I did not understand, things too wonderful for me, which I do not know. "Please listen, and I will speak; I will ask You, and You instruct me." I have heard of You by the hearing of the ear; but now my eye sees You; therefore I retract, and I repent, sitting on dust and ashes.* (Job 42:2–6)

Turns out, owning God's omnipotence and our total dependence on Him is key to a deepening relationship with Him because it positions us to encounter Him. James puts it this way: "*Come close to God and He will come close to you*" (James 4:8).

God drawing near to us?! Isn't that what we want? We can have it. It's our inheritance as children of God. The rich prayer life we long to experience flourishes in humility's soil and invites Him to draw near.

DESPITE HIS STRONG FAITH, AFTER JOB HAD IT ALL AND LOST IT ALL, HE STILL NEEDED A PIECE OF HUMBLE PIE FROM GOD.

So, yes, there will be days when the Lord feels near. Give thanks. There will be days when the Lord feels far away. Give thanks. Name everything you can think of and everything you should've already returned thanks for and haven't. As Mama might say, "It's best to stay caught up with your thank-you notes, but it's never too late to catch up, and there's never a better time to begin than now." Remember, *"The Lord is near to all who call on him, to all who call on him in truth"* (Psalm 145:18 NIV). The only moment we earthbound saints have to connect with God ... is this one.

Hugs,
Shellie

Pray with Me

Dear Lord, thank You for the gift of life. I thank You for every blessing I can see, taste, and touch and those I can't. You are the source of every good gift. I acknowledge that I am wholly dependent upon You for the air in my lungs and the gravity holding my feet to this planet. Thank You for creating the conditions necessary for life and for sustaining me through them. You are God alone. I am Your child, and today, I choose to embrace the humility that comes with my total dependence on You. I give You thanks for all the gifts of common grace I'm experiencing as I move through this day, and I thank You always and forever for Your amazing grace that has saved my soul. Be nearer still, Lord Jesus. Your servant is listening.

Practice with Me

If you don't have access to an old hymn book, search online for the lyrics to the old nineteenth century hymn "Count Your Blessings" by Johnson Oatman Jr. and fill in the blanks below. Afterward, let's record some of the many blessings surrounding us today.

When upon life's billows you are tempest tossed, when you are discouraged, thinking _____ ____ ______. Count your many blessings, name them ______ by ______, and it will surprise you what the Lord _________ _________.

Father God, today I want to thank You for:

PRAYER HABIT #10

EMBRACE THE DIVIDENDS OF PRAYING WITH FRIENDS—AND STRANGERS!

~HUGS, SHELLIE

10

OUR FATHER

Habit #10 – Embrace the dividends of praying with friends—and strangers!

The smartwatch on my wrist began to beep, reminding me it was time to pray. I hit the stop button and briefly wondered what I should do next. The three men standing in my kitchen that winter day were acquaintances who would become friends over the next six months because protracted remodeling projects can do that. The guys were present to discuss a kitchen remodel that morphed into a multi-room makeover before it was done. Granted, such circumstances can also produce hard feelings between all involved, but thankfully, that wasn't our experience. Phil and I would recommend Don Green and his guys to anyone. They were honest and hardworking on top of being flat out fun to have around, and goodness knows, remodeling projects need boatloads of good humor. But again, this was our initial meeting and my first opportunity to tell someone other than family and close friends about my prayer alerts. I dove in before I could second-guess it.

"So," I began, "my phone was going off just now to remind me to say the Lord's Prayer. It's something my friends and I are doing together. Y'all can join me if you'd like." I closed my eyes and took off without waiting for a response, "Our Father who art in heaven..." As I prayed, I could hear deep voices joining with mine ever so quietly and then adding their amens as we closed. I looked up in time to see all three men replacing their caps. The prayer break had lasted less than a minute and we went right back to business, but I feel the impact of that moment even now. It was my first time to stop and pray with *strangers*, but it hasn't been my last because the joy from this practice has so unexpectedly enriched my life. And to think, it all started with a challenge...

Of course, I took that initial challenge as more of a double-dog dare. It's how I hear things. Blame my raising. The double-dog dares of my childhood have marked me for a lifetime. This one came out of a Bible study called "The Gospel on the Ground" by Kristi McLelland.[6] I was leading the class at my home church. (If you haven't found Kristi's work, look her up. You'll enjoy her personality and her teaching, and more importantly, she'll help you fall deeper in love with Jesus!) Kristi was teaching on the growth of the early church and how the gospel spread after Christ's resurrection and ascension. You can read more on the topic in *Gospel on the Ground*, but I'll recap briefly to suit our purposes.

Early church persecution and the temple's destruction scattered Christ's followers throughout the known world. Deprived of the solace found in each other's physical nearness, these believers began practicing fixed times of prayer to stay connected. A persecuted believer stopping to pray in Samaria would draw strength from knowing her brothers and sisters in places like Rome, Judea,

---

6. Kristi McLelland, *The Gospel on the Ground* (Nashville, TN: Lifeway Press, 2022).

and Corinth were praying too. To quote Kristi, "They shared time when they could no longer share space." Isn't that beautiful?

Kristi challenged us to spend a week with this practice by setting our phone alerts to 9:00 a.m., 12:00 noon, and 3:00 p.m. and praying the Lord's Prayer together when our alarms sounded. Our class embraced the idea. I found that stopping to pray and knowing my Jesus friends were praying at the same time was very encouraging. Several years later, I'm still using these prayer alerts, albeit in a variety of ways. I'll explain that in a moment. First, let me share a little more on why I haven't let the practice go.

INVITING PEOPLE TO PRAY WITH YOU CAN BRING SWEET MOMENTS AND THE PROMISE OF A HEAVENLY HARVEST.

At the onset, I couldn't have imagined what lay ahead when I began inviting people into public prayer moments like the one I shared with my contractor and his men. I had no idea people from all walks of life would be willing to join me at a moment's notice—and yet that's precisely what has happened, time and again. I've extended prayer invitations in all sorts of situations, to seat mates barreling with me through God's big blue sky, to employees in big box home improvement stores looking to sell me an appliance, to customers waiting with me in checkout lines. I've only had one person decline to pray with me. Ravi and I were sharing a long flight when my prayer alert sounded, so I invited him into the moment.

Ravi told me he was Hindu and he was hesitant about praying together, so I prayed quietly but afterward, I realized something interesting had happened. My invite had opened a door between us. For the next couple of hours, Ravi and I got to know each other. Ravi was a brilliant young man who had originally planned on being an astrophysicist before settling on engineering. When we met, Ravi was being wooed by colleges across the States. I can't program my way out of a wet paper bag, I was on my way to speak to a ladies' group about Jesus, and I was old enough to be Ravi's mother. We could not have had less in common and yet, surprisingly, we thoroughly enjoyed learning about each other's lives and beliefs. Ravi and I were poles apart on Jesus and who we believe Him to be. I say Jesus is the one and only Son of God. Ravi believes Jesus was a great spiritual teacher. We found each other's company pleasant nonetheless, and we've stayed in touch. Who knows the Lord's purpose in our meeting? Our stories are still being written.

People may pray under their breath or not at all, but apart from Ravi, everyone else I've invited to pray has joined me. Perhaps it's because most people are at least semi-familiar with the Lord's Prayer. They may not remember all the words, but they're fairly sure it has an open and a close. That might suggest I'm not going to pull them into an open-ended revival service and lend to their willingness. Who knows? Whatever their reasons, praying with the public has afforded me the sweetest moments with people I may never have connected with otherwise, and I believe these moments are seeds capable of yielding a harvest I may not see this side of heaven.

Recently, my prayer alert sounded while I was visiting with a Jesus friend in the produce department of a large grocery store, so I wasn't at all shocked when she accepted my invite to pray. However, opening my eyes at "amen" to discover half a dozen other shoppers had paused to join us was the kind of sweet surprise that leaves an impression on a person's heart, and it's happened repeatedly.

These experiences with both friends and strangers continue to encourage my faith and strengthen my prayer life. That's why I'm eager to share them with you. Until now, we've been talking about personal prayer and learning how to come into the presence of God and enjoy Him privately, in our own space. I understand if you're thinking I've taken a surprising turn into something you don't know if you'll ever be able to do, but please stay with me.

There's treasure here. You may not ever see yourself praying with strangers, but you can and you should pray with believing friends. Why? That's a big question. I won't be able to cover it entirely because the answer is even bigger. I would argue it's God-sized! The first and best reason to pray in faith with other believers is the simplest and most obvious: Because Jesus modeled it.

As I've already noted, the first prayer I began inviting people to share with me is what many in the church refer to as the Lord's Prayer. Some believers will recognize it as the "Our Father." By either name, it comes from the instruction Jesus gave His disciples when they asked Him to teach them how to pray. The men had walked with Jesus long enough to recognize that prayer was particularly important to Him, and by this time, they had heard Him pray many times. Here are a few examples of His prayers they had witnessed:

> *I thank you, Father, Lord of heaven and earth, that you have hidden these things from the wise and understanding and revealed them to little children; yes, Father, for such was your gracious will.* (Matthew 11:25–26 ESV)

> *Father, I thank you that you have heard me. I knew that you always hear me, but I said this for the benefit of the people standing here, that they may believe that you sent me.*
> (John 11:41–42 NIV)

In fact, Luke tells us Jesus had just finished praying to His Father when the disciples petitioned Him to teach them to pray. Jesus didn't respond by telling them to address God as He had, individually and personally. Instead, He instructed the men to pray collectively. Sit with that thought for a minute and then let's read Luke 11:2–4 (NKJV) together:

> *So He said to them, "When you pray, say:* ***Our*** *Father in heaven, hallowed be Your name. Your kingdom come. Your will be done on earth as it is in heaven. Give* ***us*** *day by day our*

> *daily bread. And forgive* **us** *our sins, for* **we** *also forgive everyone who is indebted to* **us**. *And do not lead* **us** *into temptation but deliver* **us** *from the evil one."*

I added the bold emphasis. *Our, us,* and *we* are all plural pronouns. Am I suggesting we should never go to God without going to Him corporately? Absolutely not! There are far too many scriptural examples of believers calling out to God individually to draw such a sweeping conclusion and I would fight a big old grizzly bear to hold on to my one-on-one time with Jesus. That said, Jesus had purpose in teaching the disciples to address God corporately. Our Lord knows there are advantages to acknowledging that we're part of something bigger than ourselves. We're born again individually, but we're meant to experience this new life in Christ in community, as a family of believers.

Scores of books have been written by noted theologians on the importance of corporate prayer meetings. This is not that discussion. While I'd love to see all of our church gatherings become prayer meetings like the early church, rather than simply holding a midweek prayer service, I have my own reason for encouraging believers to pray together. The shared prayer challenge I've been discussing here has helped crystallize it for me, and it's the crux of this chapter's prayer habit. Simply put, *praying with other believers stimulates our own faith.*

YOU AND I AREN'T STRAY SHEEP, TRYING OUR INDIVIDUAL BEST TO LEARN THE WAYS OF OUR SHEPHERD. WE'VE BEEN BROUGHT INTO THE SHEEPFOLD TO GROW TOGETHER!

The truth is, we have to be intentional about embracing our brothers and sisters in the body of Christ because it's totally countercultural. Our society celebrates personal drive and independent effort. We touched on this in chapter 4. A pioneering, persevering mindset can be healthy—*if* it's wholly submitted to Christ. A strong individual work ethic drives entrepreneurs, launches companies, and develops innovations that improve life for all of us. But where our go-it-alone, independent, me-do-it mentality is set forth as the way to grow closer to God, independent of the rest of His body of believers, it's a problem. And a serious one. We need each other. We're meant to learn together, serve together, and yes, pray together.

Scripture talks about the power of shared prayer in many places. Here's one of them: *"Again I say to you, that if two of you agree on earth about anything that they may ask, it shall be done for them by My Father who is in heaven"* (Matthew 18:19).

We tend to hear that verse as a promise that our corporate prayer gets God's attention and moves Him to action. Sometimes, we even act as if our combined request obligates Him to answer us, but that's another discussion. For now, here's my point: I believe there's something more happening when we pray together than a number of believers assembling a quorum hoping to get God's attention. I contend your prayers fortify mine, my prayers strengthen yours, and together, we help each other keep praying, trusting, and believing, and this is the faith that moves mountains.

> *And Jesus answered and said to them, "Have faith in God. Truly I say to you, whoever says to this mountain, 'Be taken up and thrown into the sea,' and does not doubt in his heart, but believes that what he says is going to happen, it will be granted to him. Therefore, I say to you, all things for which you pray and ask, believe that you have received them, and they will be granted to you."* (Mark 11:23)

The enemy wages a relentless assault of doubt on our minds, and although that doubt thrives in isolation, it takes a direct hit in the company of other believers! I'm convinced this is one of the most important reasons why we need to seek each other out for prayer. Not to fill a quota or adhere to a formula, but to ward off the enemy and encourage one another's faith. You and I aren't stray sheep, trying our individual best to learn the ways of our Shepherd. We've been brought into the sheepfold, and we are most definitely stronger together. Stay in touch, little sheep. I'm here for you.

Hugs,
Shellie

Pray with Me

Dear Lord, community can be so messy and I can be so busy. Sometimes it just seems easier to seek You for myself and my family and avoid interacting with other believers. I hear You calling me out of this go-it-alone mentality where it comes to my faith. I know I'm guilty of pulling aside when I need to pull together. Forgive me. I want to grow closer to You and I want a stronger prayer life, so I'm ready to learn how to walk closer with other believers. Would you help me and strengthen my resolve? In your sweet name I pray, Jesus. Amen.

Practice with Me

It's challenge time! Find at least one person who will agree to pray with you this next week. Decide on your prayer times, meaning whether you choose once a day or several times a day, and set phone alerts to remind you. Record their name and your own as a commitment below, then record your experiences. I'm praying for you and with you!

Your prayer partner

Your name

Record your experiences from this week of shared prayer.

PRAYER HABIT #11

GOD BLESSES RHYTHM AND ROUTINE AS LONG AS HIS SPIRIT IS LEADING IT!

~HUGS, SHELLIE

11

ON PLANNING TO PRAY

Habit #11 – God blesses rhythm and routine as long as His Spirit is leading it!

Surprise! There will be no story time to open this chapter. My instincts are to dive straight into the deep end with this one. We're going to take a practical look at one of the challenges that awaits anyone who sets out to become a person of prayer, and for the life of me, I can't come up with an entertaining way of getting into it. In fact, I've got some questions for you that may feel like ripping off a bandage. Brace yourself. Here we go:

- You may have sung God's praises already today, or thanked Him for a hundred and one blessings, but have you prayed for the sick? (James 5:14)
- And how about the lost? You prayed for them, right? (Romans 10:1)
- I'm sure you've confessed your sins and prayed for your personal needs. You asked for your daily bread, I assume. And for God's kingdom to come? And for guidance? And for help avoiding temptation? And to be delivered from evil? (Matthew 6:9–13)

- But have you prayed for your enemies? (Matthew 5:44)
- What about church leaders? You've prayed for them, right, and for those in authority in our government? (1 Timothy 2:1–2)
- How about Israel? Have you prayed for Jerusalem? (Psalm 122:6)
- No doubt you've prayed for your immediate circle of family and friends, for your kids and grandkids and their growth in the faith. (Colossians 1:9–10)
- But what about all the tragedies around the world? And the natural disasters? And… and… and…

Hit the brakes!

I could be wrong, but I dare say none of us have been able to cover all those topics today, or any day, and just hearing that litany of petitions was overwhelming. Right? And yet, as evidenced by the Scriptures I noted with each one, we're instructed to pray for all of them. If this opening has made you feel like throwing in the prayer towel, breathe. Gulp some water, or pour yourself a cup of coffee, just please don't shut this book. I'm on mission to help people pray, not to add to anyone's guilt over not praying. And I'm here to keep pointing us all back to Holy Spirit, for He is the only One who can break the ugly guilt of prayer shaming and keep us from returning to its trap.

SPIRIT-LED ORDER IN PRAYER CAN CALM THE CHAOS AND KEEP US FROM BEING OVERWHELMED.

Trying not to neglect any of those prayer needs used to leave me feeling defeated too. I was just beginning to escape performance religion. I was discovering the joy of being friends with

God, and I was learning that anything He asks of us is ultimately for us, so I wanted to pray about everything He wanted me to pray about! Only whenever I tried to cover all the things all the time, my prayers turned back into the kind of dry, cover-the-list petitions that threatened to drain the budding intimacy with God I was tasting. Oh, no! "911, Heaven Help!"

I began asking Holy Spirit to show me a better way, and He did. I believe He inspired the idea I'm going to give to you. It's not meant to be a new rule or doctrine. My goal is to open your mind to new possibilities. Holy Spirit may show you a completely different way to address all the areas of prayer we mentioned earlier. He is personal with each of us, and we don't want to pray like anyone else, remember? Ask, seek, knock. Listen to Him and be led by Him. You'll find Him faithful. He can't be anything else, and the only path worth following is the one He is forging. What follows is how He has led me.

When I first began asking Holy Spirit to teach me how to balance all these biblical admonitions to pray, while continuing to keep company with Him, I was under the impression prayer had to be spontaneous to be spiritual. God had been teaching me that He wasn't a form to follow, steps to take, or a process to work. I was sold on that truth, and I was growing increasingly hungry for His presence. As a result, I was running hard and fast from any prayer that had the slightest procedural whiff to it. I don't remember how this *opening* in my spirit happened. I wish I could. All I can tell you is God helped me understand I was throwing the baby out with the bath water, tossing the wheat out with the chaff, burning the house down to kill the mice. Choose your idiom but hear the message that finally got through to me: *It didn't have to be all or nothing. Routine and order can be Spirit-led too!*

I began to understand that habits in prayer aren't wrong, and they can actually help us learn to pray. The danger we need to guard against is letting our prayers themselves become procedural, led by us and not Holy Spirit. Over time, I began to understand the difference. God loves routine and order—as long as He is the one leading it, as the Bible clearly demonstrates!

Consider His work of creation. From the opening words of Genesis, we're introduced to the God of order. From separating light and night in day one to resting from His work on day seven, we see God intentionally designing and creating order for His world. He spoke patterns into existence at the beginning of time that continue in the same routine today. *"As long as the earth endures, seedtime and harvest, cold and heat, summer and winter, day and night will never cease"* (Genesis 8:22 NIV).

Beyond the inherent witness of the structured world around us, I can confidently proclaim that God loves order because our very bodies brim with a host of systems that are meant to do the same seemingly monotonous jobs all day, every day. These systems continually repeat identical tasks with divinely inspired consistency that keeps us alive. Indeed, any way you cut it, that's structure on top of structure, order upon order! And God says it is *"very good"* (Genesis 1:31)! We can add our amen to the psalmist's conclusion, *"I praise you because I am fearfully and wonderfully made"* (Psalm 139:14 NIV).

And previously noted in these pages, my math skills are questionable. Thankfully, it doesn't take a scientist or engineer to see mathematical order in nature. There are recurring designs and patterns wherever we look. Every new life is a miracle, and yet each one follows the established rhythms of birth, growth, reproduction, and aging that have been repeated countless times before.

It was finally occurring to me that if God's creation runs by rules, I could rest in the knowledge that forms in themselves aren't bad, and perhaps Holy Spirit wanted to show me how to use them. So what did I do with this revelation that shouldn't have taken so long to dawn on me? (Your fellow sojourner can be a slow one!) I went to God with it. I asked Him to show me a way to heed all the biblical instructions to pray for all the needs in my circle and the world around me without losing the intimacy in prayer I was discovering. And God graciously answered. I was inspired to create a weekly prayer calendar. I took each day of the week and assigned it a biblical focus. I originally created this outline in my iPhone's notepad so it would be handy, but I've used this routine for years now, and over time it has become such an ingrained part of my prayer life that I don't need to refer to the schedule.

Another word of caution before we proceed. Though each day of my week does have its own focus as I'm about to show you, I never open my prayer time with that day's petition. I could and I would if Holy Spirit led me to, but generally speaking, my heart is set on communion as soon as my eyes open, and I beseech you to start there too. We need the enabling power of Holy Spirit to pray. If we ask Him to help us pray, He will. Otherwise, we'll have nothing to offer but dry sessions and emptier words.

So, yes, the first thing I want to do is reach for God through Christ our Savior. I want to bring my own heart to Him for cleansing. I want to praise Him and worship Him. Sitting with Him, listening for His precious voice of personal instruction, correction, and direction is my goal. How long does this communion last? That time frame varies and I'm intentionally refraining from being any more specific in case there is someone like *old legalistic Shellie* reading this. I wouldn't want anyone to get all twisted up trying to comply with directions Holy Spirit isn't giving. At some point during our fellowship, however, my thoughts will turn to the day's focus, and I will ask Holy Spirit to direct me in how to pray for it.

My prayers for these different focuses change weekly with Holy Spirit's leading. I depend on the Lord to help me keep listening for Him and alert me if I start falling into the trap of reciting old prayers. I don't want to intercede over this Tuesday's focus the same way I prayed over it the Tuesday before! For me, asking Holy Spirit to speak to me about that day's focus and depending on His direction guards against spiritless praying and helps me intercede with my heart.

My Personal Prayer Calendar

Here's a look at how my prayer calendar is organized.

Mondays

I like to begin the week praying for families. God loves family! He is the Savior of the whole world, but He established a family through Abraham, so that through their lineage, Christ came to reconcile Jew and gentile to Himself! So I pray for Israel, per Scripture's instructions. I pray for Jewish souls to come to know Jesus the Messiah, the fulfillment of God's every promise to them, and I intercede for Israel to experience peace within her borders. Then I pray for my immediate and extended family members. I ask God to draw those who don't believe to Jesus, and I pray for the growth and maturity of those who do know Him. And, of course, I'll pray for whatever physical needs my loved ones are facing.

Tuesdays

I pray for those in crisis. I created this wide-open category to cover everything from individual health concerns to wars and weather disasters. My goal is to listen for direction and pray for whoever and whatever the Lord lays on my heart. That said, some of the things that always find their way to this day's requests are my prayers for the persecuted church, for the abused and trafficked, and for those with pressing physical needs.

Wednesdays

I'm always praying for unbelievers to come to Christ, but I'm particularly intentional about it on Wednesdays. Sometimes I bring specific names to the Lord. Some days, I'm led to pray for entire cities or nations. Either way, my Wednesday prayer focus is for those who don't know Jesus and are headed into an eternity without Him. I pray for the growth of the kingdom of God and for the light of the glorious gospel to shine in dark hearts. I pray for new tongues to give Him praise, and I ask the Lord to grant me the gift of evangelism because I want to be a part of this great harvest!

Thursdays

I love to intercede for the body of Christ on Thursdays. Holy Spirit always leads me to pray for our growth and maturity. I ask the Lord to grant Christians an ever-increasing hunger for His Word and His presence. I find the apostle Paul's prayers for believers to be great aids as I pray for both the local church and the global church. Among his many requests for other believers, Paul prayed for the church to grow in wisdom and knowledge, to walk in love, to know peace and joy, to endure, and to be bold in proclaiming the gospel!

Fridays

I pray for two groups of those in authority on Friday: those in government and leaders in the body of Christ. In the first group, I cover local officials, national leaders, and others who govern or enforce the law. The second group includes everyone from pastors, teachers, and evangelists to worship leaders, youth ministers, the heads of women's groups, vacation Bible school leaders if it's that time of the year, and influencers. Again, I most often begin locally, praying for my own pastor and other ministers I know personally, before covering the broader church.

Saturdays

I pray for people in religious services around the globe on Saturdays. I usually begin with services that are gathering in the name of Jesus. I'll pray for the hearts of all who attend. I'll pray for Jesus to be celebrated and His gospel to be proclaimed in its entirety. I also pray that the light of the glorious gospel of Christ would break into the midst of groups that are being fed lies, where hate is glorified, and demonic doctrines are taught.

Sundays

I love the encouragement I get from fellowshipping with other believers. On Sundays, I pray for and with my local church or alongside any other church where I happen to be visiting or ministering. It's rare for me not to be at a church service somewhere!

PRAYING FOR SPECIFIC NEEDS EACH DAY OF THE WEEK ENABLES YOU TO BRING MANY THINGS TO GOD WITHOUT BEING OVERWHELMED.

As I said earlier, I hold this calendar loosely. It's not a system chiseled in stone. But it is an effective way for me to take a ton of loved ones and a lot of very important situations to God's throne without getting overwhelmed by the sheer volume and responsibility of it all. Still, there are mornings when my phone begins buzzing with serious needs and prayer requests before I've had time to pour a cup of coffee and sit with God. You too? Of course, I take these immediate needs to Father God, as the Spirit leads, regardless of whether the request coordinates with the day's *assigned focus* in my prayer calendar! But having this method of prayer has helped me in so many ways.

For instance, I never want to tell someone I'll be praying for them and then forget to intercede, but it can easily slip my mind. This is a way of guarding against that forgetfulness. If I've told a friend I'll pray for her as she prepares to speak at an upcoming conference, I'll associate her request with Fridays when I pray for leaders and those in authority. If someone asks me to pray for their loved one who is battling cancer, I'll associate that need with Tuesday's crisis focus. I may be interceding for them on other days too, but having them linked with a particular focus helps keep them on my heart and in my prayers.

I don't do any of this perfectly, but Father God sees my heart's intention to pray in obedience to His Word. And here's one of the principles He has taught me over and again: He will always enable and empower the steps we make toward Him.

> *He has told you, mortal one, what is good; and what does the* Lord *require of you but to do justice, to love kindness, and to walk humbly with your God?* (Micah 6:8)

To recap? We don't have to be wary of habits or routines as long as Holy Spirit is getting to lead. We can embrace them for our good and His glory!

Hugs,
Shellie

Pray with Me

Dear Lord, we praise You for the order in our universe. Help us to see where organization can aid us as we seek You. We want to be people of prayer, intercessors at Your holy throne, making our requests to You for Your purposes according to Your will. Show each of us how to establish our own prayer rhythms with You. God of all creation, we trust You to continue to teach us how to be with You in prayer and still be able to bring the needs of our whole world and our loved ones to You. For there is healing and hope in the name of Jesus, Your Son and our Savior. Amen.

Practice with Me

Read Numbers 6:23–26. What did God tell the sons of Israel to say over their people in verses 24–26? Record it below. These words are a prayer of blessing for our people. The Lord is telling the Israelites to live repeating them over their families. We're meant to do likewise. Let's start today!

PRAYER HABIT #12

FAKE PRAYING MAY BE EASIER BUT REAL WORDS DEVELOP INTIMACY WITH GOD.

~HUGS, SHELLIE

12

DON'T PRAY IT SAFE

Habit #12 – Fake praying may be easier but real words develop intimacy with God.

As I'm sure you've heard, research has proven women speak twice as many words in a day as their men do. That little fact has been well documented in the news and my own personal experience attests to it. Actually, I'm pretty sure my beloved farmer rarely uses his daily quota. Phil would probably tell you this has served him well during our many years together and I talk enough for both of us. Both of these things may be accurate, but neither of them explain why a man can get into twice the trouble with less than half as many words. For illustration, I give you the following account from one of our road trips. It's one of those funny stories our family has told and keeps telling, but it never fails to get a laugh, and it will be new to you.

The man and I were headed down Interstate 20. Phil was driving and I was working on my laptop when I mentioned there was an item in the backseat I needed. For reasons Phil can't explain to this very day, he replied, "Well, climb your big booty back there and get it."

Every female who hears those words or reads them can zero in on the three-letter word in Phil's comment that spelled trouble for my man.

"Big?" I asked, wearing my best "would you like to reconsider your statement?" expression.

In the farmer's defense, I think he really did wish he had gone in a different direction with his comment, only the more he tried to explain it was just an expression and was meant to be funny, the more tickled he got. The twinkle in his blue eyes gave it away. Fortunately for Phil, watching him trying not to laugh got me to giggling. Humor for the win again.

Even though my beloved is known in our circles for being a man of few words and I can usually find more than my share, prayer has a way of bringing us both to the same place. I think it's a spot you're familiar with too. We can all struggle to find the words we're searching for, just when we need them the most. If you get that, I want you to know God has got you! The Bible holds words we don't even know we're looking for until we find them, and they were penned by biblical writers who lived centuries before us. You and I can't even imagine the things these ancient scribes saw and heard and yet we can find our hearts in their words in classic examples of "I couldn't have said it better myself." Hello, Holy Spirit.

Friend, I suspect you're still in these pages with me because you want the same thing I do. You want to walk and talk with God without all the pretense and posturing that can so easily define your prayers. If I'm right, you're going to want to lean in for this discussion. It's doubtful any book of the Bible can help us in this quest to be real with God more than the Psalms. If there's an emotion not covered in the Psalms, I can't imagine what it would be. The Psalms were written as a book of songs, and these old tunes speak to the entire spectrum of our human experience.

I won't be surprised if we get to heaven and discover the famous nineteenth-century American poet Henry Wadsworth

Longfellow had been reading in the Psalms when he noted, "Music is the universal language of mankind." The songs of Psalms document everything from the wildest expressions of joy to grief's raw wailings. Heartache and happiness, anger, regret, and guilt, confusion and disappointment—it's all there. But it's how these emotions are processed that can energize our prayer lives. Consider reading the following bullet points several times over and asking the good Lord to plant them deep in your heart. I'm listing them like this because I can't overemphasize how these truths can help us learn to pray.

- No one in the Psalms seems to be praying the prayers they think God wants to hear!
- The Psalms are full of very real people bringing their very real lives to God.
- The psalmists want to hear from God, so they make sure God hears from them!

These early believers don't doctor or decorate their words when they reach for God. They bring Him who they are, where they are, and exactly what's bothering them, even if, and maybe especially when, what's upsetting them the most is God's seeming indifference to their pain! Whoa. That's nervy, right? It might be in our book, but it doesn't read that way in God's.

Fake praying is so much easier than real praying. My definition of fake praying is when what we're saying with our mouths has no connection to how we're feeling in our hearts. We can fake pray our entire believing lives away stringing together holy sounding sentences and pretty phrases we've learned at church. The sad truth is we'll get exactly nowhere. Fake praying accomplishes nothing, and it brings us no closer to our heart's desire to know God!

Can we be honest with ourselves about why we lean on fake praying? It's clean, tidy, and totally doable. We can *say our prayers* without ever truly engaging with God. We can offer Him what we think He wants to hear while stuffing away how we really feel and hide the fact that our hearts are mouthing different words than our lips. "Do you really care about what's happening to me here..." Oh, no. We keep those real words choked back because that type of honesty is uncomfortable, and it can be downright intimidating. We sense the open-ended drama those real words might lead to and we're hesitant to go there. (Who has time for that, right?) We're far more comfortable with our practiced prayers because we get to start them, and we get to end them, on our own terms with a nice Christian amen. Daily devotion? Check. Prayers? Check. No risk, no reward.

On the other hand, real praying is as messy as fake praying is neat, but it's where we encounter God. And it's these sacred meetings that stir our hearts for more of Him.

REAL WORDS EQUAL HUMILITY, AND HUMBLE HUMANS ENCOUNTER GOD.

Going there with God and opening up to Him doesn't always change the situation, but real praying never fails because we get Father's ear and His presence changes us. When we pour our hearts out with God day after day after day, He begins to transform us in ways that can escape us in the moment. We seldom see His line upon line, plank by plank remodeling of our lives ... until the day it becomes obvious, even to us, that all our reaching for Him, every awkward little grasp, has been molding us and remaking us. When we begin to see what God has been doing, no one is more surprised than we are to discover that all the times we have dared to say what we were really feeling have changed us, are changing us, and this realization makes us want to go to Him more.

Confession? As much as I love prayer now, getting past fake prayers and into real ones can still challenge me. My confidence to keep pressing in lies with knowing God wants this intimacy with me more than I could ever desire it of Him and He has made provision for it. Thank You, Lord! In the next chapter, I'll share what helps me move into real words. For now, let's stay here and learn more about the benefits of discovering how to recognize and move past fake praying. This is where the records of those biblical believers we mentioned earlier who dared to open their hearts to God can prove so valuable to us. We have much to gain from their experiences!

Sometimes, after these saints pour their hearts out to God, we notice a shift in their prayers, and we get to see how processing with God has begun to reframe the situation for them and open their understanding. In these accounts, we're treated to their newfound wisdom in the same passage that holds their transparent cries. Yes! We love that, right? Timely wisdom, instant clarity! We want that! Other times, we get no such takeaway. We watch these believers unload their hearts and we're right there with them, holding our breath at their audacity, waiting for God to move. Only they get nothing. We don't like it near as much when the Bible leaves all their feelings right there, delivered and met with heavenly silence, but there's truth for us here too.

For His own good reasons, God chose to include these seemingly unanswered prayers in His Book, and in doing so, He validated their messy prayers as surely as He did the others. Why? I don't have a one-size-fits-all answer to that question, but I'll share one of my working theories. Maybe God put their prayers into His permanent record to show us, His beloved kids who want our questions answered yesterday, that He is saving all our tears and recording all our cries, even those we feel sure have fallen to the ground! God's silence challenges our faith, and He knows it. It confronts us. It requires us to choose whether we'll be offended by His decision not to speak or stand on what He has already revealed. The good news is that if we decide, come what may, we're going to plant our shaky feet in the truth of God and trust Him in the deafening silence, we get to experience the solid rock beneath them. Praise Him! Let's explore this further by looking at Psalm 13.

Some theologians believe the author of this psalm was King Solomon, while others believe it was his father, King David. Regardless of who penned it, the words of this hymn sound like lyrics any of us could have written at one time or another. I'm glad God preserved them. In addition to having a good example of a prayer that doesn't hold back, we get a front-row seat to what happens in the author's heart after he pours it out before God.

> *How long, LORD? Will You forget me forever? How long will You hide Your face from me? How long am I to feel anxious in my soul, with grief in my heart all the day? How long will my enemy be exalted over me? Consider and answer me, O LORD my God; enlighten my eyes, or I will sleep the sleep of death, and my enemy will say, "I have overcome him," and my adversaries will rejoice when I am shaken.* (Psalm 13:1–4)

No need to ask the writer how he really feels. There's no fake praying in that passage. In case you weren't counting, there were four *how long am I going to have to endure this* complaints in two verses. I've felt that. You? And yet, if we keep reading, we'll find the psalmist joyfully reassuring himself of the faithfulness of his God, the very One he has just accused of leaving him at the mercy of his enemy! Take these next lines in and meet me below.

> *But I have trusted in Your faithfulness; my heart shall rejoice in Your salvation. I will sing to the LORD, because He has looked after me.* (Psalm 13:5–6)

Something has happened between the *how long* accusations levied against God that we find in the opening verses, and the author's stated intention in verse six to break into song. We're not given the details behind his dramatic mood swing, but there's clearly been a change of heart. So why did he cancel his pity party anyway? A host of biblical scholars much smarter than I have tried to answer that question but I'll take a turn at it.

I believe the shift in the writer's perspective is directly connected to the way he was praying. The doubts he had been entertaining lost their steam at the throne. The enemy's lies crumbled in the presence of God who is truth and who states in Proverbs 8:14 (NKJV), *"Counsel is mine, and sound wisdom; I am understanding, I have strength."* I believe it was the psalmist's honesty that positioned him to be counseled from heaven. Now his faith is renewed. Suddenly, he can remember the past times God has been faithful to him and he is encouraged to believe God will be faithful to him again. And why? Because *"The LORD is near to all who call on him, to all who call on him **in truth**"* (Psalm 145:18 NIV). Don't miss those last two words.

Almighty God is drawn to humble humans. Read this passage from James 4:6–8 (NKJV) with me:

> *But He gives more grace. Therefore He says: "God resists the proud, but gives grace to the humble." Therefore submit to God. Resist the devil and he will flee from you. Draw near to God and He will draw near to you.*

If we're longing for true intimacy with God, we must grasp this truth. Our enemy will let us spend as much time as we care to invest in our independent, self-driven, boundary-established fake praying that sounds nice and churchy to our prideful ears. In fact, I wouldn't be surprised if the devil actually encourages fake praying because it allows him to plant his ugly thoughts in our heads, lies we easily mistake for our own. See if you recognize any of them: "Either God isn't listening, or He doesn't care. ... Maybe He isn't even real..."

The enemy doesn't have to win. We can take this weapon out of his hands! Real words equal humility and humble humans encounter God. Now that you know, what will you do with this revelation?

Hugs,
Shellie

Pray with Me

Dear Lord, I am hungry for You. I don't want to use fake prayer words, but I confess that I often do because they're easier! Teach me how to pray with my whole heart. Help me break this old pattern. Alert me when I'm holding myself apart from You and simply going through the motions. I know You see my thoughts. Give me the courage to voice them. In the sweet name of Jesus, I pray. Amen.

Practice with Me

Identify an area of your life where you need to hear from God. Pen a prayer about it using real words.

PRAYER HABIT #13

PRAY WITH GOD'S OWN WORDS; THEY NEVER FAIL!

~HUGS, SHELLIE

13

YOU CAN SAY THAT AGAIN

Habit #13 – Pray with God's own words; they never fail!

My goals in elementary school were simple enough. I wanted to have a good time while entertaining my classmates. Smiles were good; laughs were better. My teachers did not share my aspirations, and unfortunately for me, I knew getting in trouble at school meant additional trouble at home. Should my sisters and I find ourselves on a teacher's bad side, we knew our parents wouldn't consider us innocent until proven guilty. That's a nice concept, but Ed and Charlotte's tendency leaned more toward authority being right until authority was proven wrong. I tried to conform to adult expectations and I did my best to keep the clowning to a minimum but now that the statute of limitations has played out, I would like to put something on my permanent record.

There were times when I got in trouble for acting out when I was honestly trying to understand the assignment. Take those true-or-false quizzes my peers enjoyed. Those tricky tests tried my grade-school soul. Not even joking. I would get all up in my head over them. "I mean, I can tell it's false, but if it's true that it's false, does that mean the right answer is true or false?" It was a legitimate question from the vantage point of my tender years, but convincing my teacher I wasn't trying to be funny was a challenge I lost more than once, right along with my recess privileges. Sigh.

That may be one of the first times I remember having trouble understanding the assignment, but it wasn't the last, by any means. I know how frustrating it can be to want to follow directions—if only you could figure out how to participate. It's those kind of experiences that motivate my writing and speaking ministry and make me want to communicate in ways you can understand and apply to your own life. You're with me in these pages because you want to pray those real prayers we talked about in the previous chapter. In this one, I want to show you how God's Word can help us get there and I'm committed to doing it as clearly as I can.

Way back in chapter 1, I differentiated between using written prayers and praying with our own words. If you'll remember, I said I enjoy praying written prayers and I believe in their value. All true! In the last year or so, I've even found myself becoming increasingly fond of liturgical prayers, a more formal, structured style of worship often shared with other members of Christ's body. Liturgical prayers are fairly new to me. They were seldom used in the church I attended as a child, although the church I attend now has grown in this practice in recent years, largely due to one sweet saint who is relentless in beating the drum for corporate prayer. (I love you, Mrs. Ann!) My daughter-in-law also gave me a book called, *Every Moment Holy* by Douglas Kaine McKelvey.[7] (Thanks, Carey!) It's a beautiful compilation of liturgies for the ordinary events of life like folding clothes and decorating for Christmas. It's also become a favorite of mine to use when I gather family and friends at my house.

But once again, while I'm enjoying these written prayers, they haven't come close to sating my desire for personal intimacy with Jesus. I remain unsatisfied in simply reading to God. My heart

---

7. Douglas Kaine McKelvey, *Every Moment Holy, Volume I: New Liturgies for Daily Life* (Nashville, TN: Rabbit Room Press, 2017).

longs to talk with Him. You too? Good. Stay with me. Written prayers may not have been the solution to my God hunger, but they've most certainly served my prayer life, which is why I bring them into our discussion. My experience is that using God's Word in prayer is like priming a water pump. It stirs my spirit and encourages my own words to flow. Since most modern pumps are self-primed these days and not everyone grew up in the country, let's revisit my childhood again to help that analogy land.

SCRIPTURE PRIMES THE PUMP OF OUR PRAYERS, CAUSING THEM TO FLOW AND CONNECT MORE INTIMATELY WITH GOD.

I grew up on a farm in rural Louisiana. It wasn't unusual to see someone pour water down an inactive pump to get it working. As a child, I thought having to pour water *into* the pump when we were trying to get water *from* the pump was strange. To be honest, I don't understand that much more about plumbing as an adult, but I have a handle on the basics. Pouring water into the pump was about replacing the air in the pump's intake line. Those who were priming the pump were essentially filling the void until water met water and the flow began. Oh, what a beautiful way to bring us back on point.

We often come to prayer hungry for God but topped off and tapped out emotionally, pressed down and preoccupied with this world's cares. And precisely because we feel bone dry and out of commission, we'll start acting like we have to search the universe over, cross the deepest seas, and climb the highest mountains to reach our God. Silly, silly us. Holy Spirit of God lives in our hearts, and He never leaves us nor forsakes us. Our hearts just get full of other things, lesser things. Oh, that I could put a number to the many times I've been there! Longing for God but having trouble finding my way home in prayer is a quandary I know all too well.

Mark this and hold it close. I'm discovering the cure for spiritual homesickness is Jesus, always Jesus.

In John 1:1, the apostle uses these words to describe Jesus, *"In the beginning was the Word, and the Word was with God, and the Word was God."*

When we're trying to slow down from the busy pace of our lives and connect with God, praying the Word can serve to initiate the intimacy we're longing for because Jesus is the Word. He is present in the very words we're praying, and the power of His Word awakens our souls. It's often in this lingering that our own words begin to bubble up before Him. As I've already confessed, there are still days when I have trouble getting past fake praying and into authentic prayer words that go beyond surface dialogue. It happened to me just this morning! Thankfully, God has taught me that I can always *prime the pump* when I'm distracted and sluggish by praying Scripture until His Spirit touches my spirit, and my own prayer words begin to flow. This is the power of His living Word! The apostle Paul loved to speak of the power of God's Word to do in us what He wills in us. He didn't mind repeating himself and I don't either. I can't recommend the Word to you often enough!

> *So now, brethren, I commend you to God and to the word of His grace, which is able to build you up and give you an inheritance among all those who are sanctified.* (Acts 20:32 NKJV)

"The word of His grace" is able to build us up! Amen! That's my best effort at explaining how God's Word offers us an invaluable aid in kickstarting our prayers, but there are so many other ways Scripture can help us in prayer beyond being a holy fire starter.

The Word can also fuel our prayers as our communion continues. Layering our real words with Scripture as we continue to pray is like tossing the occasional log on a burning fire. It's sacred inspiration that fuels us in real time. The Word can also offer us direction as we pray over a matter, steering us into the knowledge of what to pray and growing our faith as we call out to God.

> *So then faith comes by hearing, and hearing by the word of God.* (Romans 10:17 NKJV)

Did you hear that? Faith is born in our hearts through the Word and the faith that is in our hearts grows the same way, through the Word. Praying Scripture lays hold of the God who spoke the words we're praying. He is present to start a brushfire in our prayers with His Word as the kindling. What does it look like to let God's Word fuel our words? I'm getting there. There's no way I'm leaving you here all stirred up with that promise and not addressing the how! Let's break it down.

One way we can use Scripture in our prayers is by taking what's going on in our lives and asking Holy Spirit to bring a Scripture to our mind that applies to it. Please don't get discouraged if you don't yet have enough Scripture in your heart to pull from. Yes, the goal is to hide God's Word in our hearts so we can draw on it as needed. Those who neglect God's Word will always be hampered in their prayers. And those who neglect prayer will always be hampered in their understanding of God's Word. But take heart if you've only just begun to follow Jesus. There are numerous Scripture aids to help those who are new to Bible study. You can find an applicable verse by looking up a key word in your Bible's concordance or by using one of the many Bible tools available online. You can also use a simple search engine. Angry at someone? Typing *Bible verse* and *anger* in your search query will return enough verses to get you well on your way. Once you find a verse, rewrite it into a prayer. I'll illustrate this for you.

You might find, "*A soft answer turns away wrath, but a harsh word stirs up anger*" (Proverbs 15:1 ESV). Your opening prayer could sound like this: "Dear Lord, I'm so angry right now, I can't think straight, but I don't want to make it worse by saying the wrong things. Help me choose my words and speak softly."

Another way to pray God's Word is to take a passage and rewrite it in the first person. If I want to pray for my grandchildren, I can begin with a prayer like the one Paul prayed in the first chapter of Ephesians. The original passage reads like this:

> *For this reason I too, having heard of the faith in the Lord Jesus which exists among you and your love for all the saints, do not cease giving thanks for you, while making mention of you in my prayers; that the God of our Lord Jesus Christ, the Father of glory, may give you a spirit of wisdom and of revelation in the knowledge of Him. I pray that the eyes of your heart may be enlightened, so that you will know what is the hope of His calling, what are the riches of the glory of His inheritance in the saints, and what is the boundless greatness of His power toward us who believe.* (Ephesians 1:15–19)

If I were going to use that passage to jumpstart my prayers for my grandchildren, it might sound like this:

> Father, I'm so thankful my older grandchildren have put their faith in You, and I'm trusting You to draw little Kennedy to You as soon as she understands the gospel. Would You give my grandchildren a spirit of wisdom and revelation that would allow them to increase in the knowledge of Christ? And would You help them have a growing understanding of the hope they now have in You and help them grasp the power You extend toward them because they believe?

From there, I may be prompted to begin praying about situations or challenges specific to the different grandkids, according to what's going on in their individual lives.

Another of my favorite ways to convert Scripture into prayer is by using acronyms. I've found combining several thoughts into one word helps me remember the different points. I've recently been praying for a ton of people using Philippians 1:9–11, an incredibly rich passage:

> *And this I pray, that your love may overflow still more and more in real knowledge and all discernment, so that you may discover the things that are excellent, that you may be sincere and blameless for the day of Christ; having been filled with the fruit of righteousness which comes through Jesus Christ, for the glory and praise of God.*

I've put the main ideas from that passage into the acronym *LOVE* to help me remember the different points. I'll pray for the person to:

- L - Live a pure life walking wholeheartedly with God
- O - Overflow in love from experimental knowledge of God, growing in wisdom
- V - Value what is good and best, discerning clearly
- E - Evidence fruits from a life lived with Jesus

GOD'S WORD NEVER FALLS SHORT AND NEVER FAILS.

Remembering these points helps me stay focused, but again, I rarely pray the point without enlarging on it. I've found acronyms to be incredible memory tools because they can help me pray during the day when I'm driving or involved in a task that prevents me from looking at my notes or reading my Bible. Sometimes I'll use the one above to pray for people by name; sometimes I'll pray for "my kids and my grandkids," "my parents," "my church family," or a group of people I've just spoken to at an event. It depends on where I am in my conversation with the Lord! Notice the points of my acronym are not in the same order as they are in the verses. I'm okay with that as long as the acronym helps me remember them!

When you first begin praying Scripture, you'll probably need to write the words out in a prayer journal as you're looking at the verse. However, it's been my sweet experience that with practice, it becomes increasingly natural until you're able to pray God's Word even as you're reading it! Sometimes I realize I'm doing a combination of reading and praying without intending to at all. For example, if I'm reading, "*His banner over me is love*" from Song of Solomon 2:4, I'll find myself reading it as, "*Your* banner over me is love" instead of *His* banner.

Sometimes Bible passages are already penned in first person, and the way another believer has reached out to God addresses how I'm feeling with words that are so appropriate, I'll pray them just as they're written. "*Your words were found and I ate them, and Your words became a joy to me and the delight of my heart; for I have been called by Your name, O Lord God of hosts*" (Jeremiah 15:16 AMP). That's my heart, word for word.

It's a mystery the way God's Word begins to move on my heart and cause my own authentic prayers to begin flowing, but it's a marvelous one that never ceases to amaze me. Unlike ours, God's words never fall short and they never fail. Learn to use them both as prayer starters and holy fuel to keep those prayers of yours burning! You have nothing to lose and everything to gain. Praying Scripture will help you linger before Him. It will deepen your experience of God and wonder of wonders, it will increase your longing to know Him that much more. We bring ourselves to Him, and He does the work. Selah.

Hugs,
Shellie

Pray with Me

Dear Lord, thank You for the Bible. I need wisdom and I believe holy Scripture contains the words of life. Help me to always hunger for more of it so I can know You more and so I can linger longer in prayer. When I'm filling my mind with everything but Your Word, remind me that I'm forfeiting the privilege of hearing Your counsel and being led by You in prayer. Teach me how to prioritize Bible reading. I want to hide Your Word in my heart. Help me to learn to memorize passages so I can pray Your words along with my own. In the sweet name of Jesus, Your Son and my Savior, I pray. Amen.

Practice with Me

So how are you right now? No, really. Be honest. Describe something that's going on in your life and how it is making you feel:

Now find an applicable verse using one of the tips we discussed in this chapter and turn it into your own prayer. Record it here.

PRAYER HABIT #14

SYNC YOUR PRAYERS WITH YOUR BREATHING TO DRAW NEARER TO GOD.

~HUGS, SHELLIE

14

EVERY BREATH I TAKE, EVERY PRAYER I MAKE

Habit #14 – Sync your prayers with your breathing to draw nearer to God.

It's been several decades since I've given birth but a goodly portion of those labor and delivery moments are forever seared in my memory, like having to be reminded to breathe between contractions. Prior to my first time giving birth, I had never given much thought to breathing. It was an automatic process. But having a baby in your body who is determined to get out is a life-altering experience. My prenatal care had convinced me of the advantages to deep breathing in order to *relax my pelvic floor* but when push came to shove—and I mean that quite literally—I preferred crashing between contractions and letting my pelvic floor recover on its own.

Had it not been for the sweet nurses at my side who insisted that I breathe in and breathe out slowly to get my body ready for the next contraction, my deliveries would have taken even longer, and believe me, they were lengthy enough. I'm just thrilled for the adorable pregnant girls who arrive at the hospital looking like they swallowed a soccer ball, capture a few social media reels during the action, and pose afterward with their makeup intact. (That didn't sound as sincere as I had hoped.) I, however, had a habit of staying through shift change and getting acquainted with everyone who worked in obstetrics before giving birth—and I looked like it.

We can all agree breathing is a good thing that goes beyond the benefits involved in birthing the next generation. Science has proven controlled breathing can enhance lung capacity, promote relaxation, reduce the heart rate, and lower blood pressure! Deep breathing activates the vagus nerve, which helps to regulate stress and anxiety. And by sending more oxygen to the brain, we can effectively calm ourselves down. This is where anyone who has ever tried to soothe a fitful toddler is saying, "No, duh, Shellie." I hear you. I didn't need to understand the science behind controlled breathing to tell a child in the middle of a meltdown, "Take a deep breath and let it out slowly" either. I knew it worked from experience. I have been slower in realizing the potential and value of connecting my breath with God's Word. Maybe you have been too.

I've already told you I'm not a prayer expert, teaching on prayer because I've arrived. Far from it. I'm your fellow sojourner, sharing in real time what I'm learning as I follow hard after Jesus, and this chapter's prayer habit—the practice of syncing my breath with Scriptures—is one of my more recent loves! Unlike some of the habits I've shared in earlier chapters, this is something I haven't been practicing for very long. At least not in the way I am now. More on that in just a bit. Though I'm admittedly late to the party on this one, I'm increasingly grateful to be here.

Backstory? I've always avoided using any kind of controlled breathing techniques in prayer beyond *take a breath and calm down* because of their connection to Eastern religions or practices like Hinduism, Buddhism, yoga, and Taoism. My position hasn't changed there. Deep breathing exercises that encourage self-realization and aim to control the mind and body in order to achieve a higher state of consciousness conflict with biblical views of God and Spirit led prayer. Steer clear of any *path to enlightenment* that doesn't hold up

Jesus as *"the way, and the truth, and the life"* (John 14:6). You and I are aiming to stay firmly rooted in Christ and He is the goal of breath praying.

Both Zen teachers and secular scientists believe our breath is a bridge between mind and body, but both groups fall short of truth when they don't acknowledge the almighty God who created both and linked the two. True science doesn't conflict with truth; it springs from truth. I'm reminded of a quote from famous astronomer Johannes Kepler: "O God, I am thinking Thy thoughts after Thee." The science of deep breathing exists because God does, but its value is realized only as far as it acknowledges the potential power of connecting our breath to God's Word for worship and communion.

IN BREATH PRAYING, YOU EXHALE YOUR NEEDS AND INHALE HIS PROVISION.

Christian breath praying is the practice of connecting our breath with the recitation of a simple Scripture-based prayer and as I said earlier, it may not have been on my radar, but it's not a new discipline. Christians have been using this ancient practice for centuries. Breath praying differs from the Eastern traditions we mentioned earlier in that we aren't using mantras to try and calm ourselves and we're not trying to master ourselves by emptying our minds. On the contrary, with breath prayers, we're filling our minds with God's Word and acknowledging that true peace and wisdom come from Him alone. We're owning our weakness and acknowledging our need for God's presence and His strength by meditating on truth.

> *Finally, brothers and sisters, whatever is true, whatever is honorable, whatever is right, whatever is pure, whatever is lovely, whatever is commendable, if there is any excellence and*

> *if anything worthy of praise, think about these things. As for the things you have learned and received and heard and seen in me, practice these things, and the God of peace will be with you.* (Philippians 4:8–9)

Combining our breath with God's Word is powerful. I'm enjoying it for a host of reasons that I'll share with you shortly but first, let's dig into the how-to of breath praying. As we've noted, Christian breath praying is rooted in Scripture. It's practiced by taking a Bible verse that is applicable to our present situation and breaking it down into two simple phrases that fit within a single breath. To connect the verse with our breathing, we say the first half as we inhale and the second half as we exhale. I'll give you some examples.

One of my favorite go-to verses when I'm upset is Psalm 94:19: *"When my anxious thoughts multiply within me, Your comfort delights my soul."* Using that verse as a breath prayer, I inhale with, "When I'm anxious" and exhale on, "Your comfort brings me joy."

When I'm going about my day and just wanting to reach for Jesus, I might pray Psalm 119:68. I'll inhale with, "You are good and You do good" and exhale with, "Teach me your commandments."

Sometimes I'll use a verse word for word. If I need answers, I might pull from 1 Samuel 3:9 (ESV): *"Speak, LORD, for your servant hears."* I'll inhale with, *"Speak, LORD"* and exhale on, *"for your servant hears."*

If I need provision, I may turn to Psalm 23:1 (NKJV). I'll inhale with, *"The LORD is my shepherd"* and exhale with, *"I shall not want."*

When I'm in a worship posture, I may use Psalm 89:1 (NKJV). I'll inhale with, *"With my mouth will I make known"* and exhale with, *"Your faithfulness to all generations."*

Many times, I've come to the end of my early morning time with Jesus, conscious of the need to move into the day's responsibilities but not wanting to forfeit all He is speaking to my heart. "I don't want to walk out of prayer," I'll whisper. "Help me to stay aware of You." Breath praying is answering this growing desire to "*pray without ceasing*" (1 Thessalonians 5:17) and I want you to enjoy it, too! Fun fact? The Greek translation for the familiar phrasing, "*pray without ceasing*" or "pray at all times" is *en pants kairo*, which sounds like someone spilled corn syrup on their britches but that's not it at all. *En pants kairo* actually carries the idea of "at each and every occasion, in anything and everything, in every respect and every way." You can think of it as getting up, sitting down, and walking around in constant communion with the One who gave us breath and is actively sustaining it. This is what I'm after, for His presence is life! And breath praying is one more way to pursue it.

Breath praying helps us stay connected to God as we move through the day. It can calm us down in heated moments when our own words are failing us and realign us with Jesus, who is our peace. When we've lost perspective and need direction, breath praying can bring us back to God and tune our ears to receive much needed real time wisdom. When we're blindsided by life, breath praying can quiet our fears in real time.

Through faith, we have access to all our Father is, through all Jesus has done. With breath praying, we get to exhale our needs, failures, and challenges and inhale God's wisdom, power, and provision. The breath in our lungs is God's gift to us.

> *Then the LORD God formed a man from the dust of the ground and breathed into his nostrils the breath of life, and the man became a living being.* (Genesis 2:7 NIV)

As surely as our physical bodies are lifeless without breath, our souls dry up and shrivel without prayer. Learning to take God's Word in and out with the rhythms of our breath nourishes our souls with life, God Himself.

Hugs,
Shellie

Pray with Me

Father God, we want to reach for You in our dedicated prayer times, but we also want to stay connected to You during the busyness of our days. Teach us how to sync the breath in our lungs with the life in Your Word so we can live listening for You, learning from You, and leaning on You. In the sweet name of Jesus, we pray. Amen.

Practice with Me

Find a Scripture verse that is applicable to your life. Turn it into a breath prayer and record it below.

PRAYER HABIT #15

FAITH MOVES MOUNTAINS, AND YOUR BODY CAN MOVE YOUR FAITH!

~HUGS, SHELLIE

15

THE BODY LANGUAGE OF WORSHIP

Habit #15 – Faith moves mountains, and your body can move your faith!

My husband grew up Methodist. I was raised Baptist—Southern Baptist to be exact. As newlyweds, Phil and I were trying to decide whether we were going to be Methodists or Baptists when our curiosity got piqued by a brand new nondenominational congregation in our small town. I suppose it felt like a compromise between our church traditions because we only visited a couple of times before agreeing to make it our church home. It would be nice if I could say we spent serious time seeking the Lord on this decision but that's not true. We may have offered a perfunctory prayer or two, but we were mainly drawn to Providence Church because it had more people our own age than some of the other congregations. I'm not recommending that selection process, and I'm fairly certain my Baptist parents thought we had joined a cult, but they came around ... with time. To be sure, a lot of things have changed over time.

The two of us soon became four. In the ensuing decades, we toted toddlers to Providence Church, then teens, and now we worship with older grandkids at our sides and the youngest quickly outgrowing our laps. During these years, what I want out of my relationship with God and how I worship Him have changed too. I'm thinking of one Sunday morning in particular.

We hadn't been at Providence long, and while I was enjoying a more relaxed church experience, I wasn't as comfortable with the occasional demonstrations of worship that went beyond a robust hymn and a hearty amen. That morning, a very traditional me caught a glimpse of another believer. Try to imagine this audacity—she had her hands cupped and she was holding them out as if asking the Lord to fill them. Okay, so her cupped hands were barely off her lap and a person had to be looking for this outrageous display to see it, but I was looking and she was ... well, worshipping. Oh, the gall. Right? Please don't miss my tongue planted firmly in my cheek. As embarrassing as that story is, and though I barely recognize that old me, I've got a more recent story for you from the other end of the spectrum.

The worship service at my home church was particularly anointed that Sunday morning. I had just returned from leading a super sweet ladies' conference in Somewhere, USA. And while my flesh may have been dragging from the weekend's travel, my spirit was tanked up on Jesus. My husband stood relatively still beside me, worshipping in his quiet but very sincere way. I was, shall we say, decidedly more demonstrative. At one point, with my hands reaching for the heavens, I leaned over to my man and whispered something like, "This is so good! I might have to stand on my chair!" Now, I was joking. Kinda. I mean, it was good, but I wasn't really considering standing on my chair. And yet my beloved farmer never blinked, though he is as conservative in his worship style as I am now enthusiastic. Phil didn't raise a single disproving eyebrow. He just whispered back, "Well, let me know before you do. I'll hold your chair so you don't fall." Bless him.

These two stories are quite the markers on my journey with Jesus, wouldn't you say? My exuberance for praise and worship today stands in sharp contrast to the reaction I had all those years ago when that sweet believer offered her open hands in a discreet gesture of submission. (I actually 'fessed up to her years later, and the two of us shared a laugh over it.) Regardless of whether your worship style is as outwardly enthusiastic as mine or closer to Phil's more traditional posture, I hope you give others the grace my husband gives me. For I was dead wrong in how I once judged my fellow believer!

The truth is, neither emotion nor the lack of outward expression are trustworthy indicators of where we are spiritually. Hypocrites can jump pews and the quiet worshipper who appears devout and respectful can actually be cold and unfeeling. This chapter is not about pressuring anyone into visible displays of emotion that aren't authentic. The Bible repeatedly warns us against trying to impress God or man with our worship or performing empty exhibitions. Isaiah 29:13, Ezekiel 33:31, and Matthew 15:8 are just a few of the references we'd best take seriously. My aim here is the same as it has been with all the prayer habits we've already discussed: to help you keep company with God.

I don't know what came to your mind when you read this chapter's title, but generally speaking, when we talk about the body language of worship, the first images that come to mind are the types of extremes typified in those personal stories I mentioned. If you'll let me, I want to stretch that thinking.

ALTHOUGH GOD SAYS, "BE STILL, AND KNOW THAT I AM GOD," THAT DOESN'T MEAN YOU CAN'T MOVE A MUSCLE.

My first experience in realizing that moving my body could help me pray came out of the desperation we talked about in chapter 6. I owned up to my inability to *"Be still, and know that I am God"* (Psalm 46:10 NKJV) without falling asleep. Remember? The problem was my understanding of that verse was too narrow. I thought it required me to be physically still. It sounded like someone sitting motionless with her hands folded in quiet contemplation, only when I tried that posture, I usually ended up dozing through my devotional time. Sigh.

If you can relate, I've got good news. "*Be still*" can also be translated as "quit striving," "withdraw," or "relax." This familiar encouragement is found in Psalm 46 (NKJV). Let's look at all eleven verses.

> *God is our refuge and strength, a very present help in trouble. Therefore we will not fear, even though the earth be removed, and though the mountains be carried into the midst of the sea; though its waters roar and be troubled, though the mountains shake with its swelling. Selah. There is a river whose streams shall make glad the city of God, the holy place of the tabernacle of the Most High. God is in the midst of her, she shall not be moved; God shall help her, just at the break of dawn. The nations raged, the kingdoms were moved; He uttered His voice, the earth melted. The* LORD *of hosts is with us; the God of Jacob is our refuge. Selah. Come, behold the works of the* LORD, *who has made desolations in the earth. He makes wars cease to the end of the earth; He breaks the bow and cuts the spear in two; He burns the chariot in the fire. Be still, and know that I am God; I will be exalted among the nations, I will be exalted in the earth! The* LORD *of hosts is with us; the God of Jacob is our refuge. Selah.*

Did you see it? The psalmist isn't addressing our body posture anywhere in that passage. We're being told to take a huge heavenly breath in the midst of this world's chaos and remind ourselves that God is in control. The nations are raging, earth is melting, war is everywhere, and God wants the psalmist to know that He is still in charge and He is a mighty refuge for those who seek Him. So here's your prayer tip: If it helps you to move while you're praying, by all means, move it!

These days, as soon as I realize I'm growing drowsy in prayer, I move! If I'm sitting, I may get up and stretch or physically extend my hands toward God. This looks different on different days. I might stand, kneel, or walk to a window, but I'll move toward God by moving my body as I continue to pray. And by changing my posture and reaching for God through my actions, I'm essentially yielding to His will to "love the Lord my God with all my heart, with all my soul, with all my mind, and with all my strength." (See Mark 12:30.) For the etymology of that word "strength" includes all of my ability, might, or power.

While we're talking about changing postures, let me add this. Sometimes that change of posture is as simple as dropping my chin to my chest. For years, it seemed I looked outside of me to find God, even though I know He lives within me. It occurred to me not long ago that I tend to look up and out when I pray, and that is absolutely fine. I have no plans to stop. But I'm also discovering that when I'm struggling in prayer, dropping my chin to my chest can be a sweet act that helps me connect to the One who is always with me, who will never leave me nor forsake me, and the One I don't have to cross oceans or climb mountains to find.

We're familiar with the Scripture that tells us God weaves us together in our mother's wombs. (See Psalm 139:13.) We know God reached down and formed Adam from dust. But do we ever wonder why? Why did He choose to make us embodied spirits and not just spirits? If you're waiting on me to answer that question, you'll be waiting a while. It's far above my pay grade. However, I do know God is not indifferent to our bodies. He enjoys our bodies. We can know this for He has ordained that we will worship Him in glorified bodies forever:

> *But our citizenship is in heaven. And we eagerly await a Savior from there, the Lord Jesus Christ, who, by the power that enables him to bring everything under his control, will transform our lowly bodies so that they will be like his glorious body.* (Philippians 3:20–21 NIV)

This much I can tell you with the utmost confidence: Creator God didn't design our bodies to hinder our relationship with Him! He designed them for His pleasure, and His pleasure is that we might know Him.

> *My heart is steadfast, O God! I will sing and make melody with all my being!* (Psalm 108:1 ESV)

> *My lips will shout for joy, when I sing praises to you; my soul also, which you have redeemed.* (Psalm 71:23 ESV)

> *I appeal to you … brothers, by the mercies of God, to present your bodies as a living sacrifice, holy and acceptable to God, which is your spiritual worship.* (Romans 12:1 ESV)

Prayer isn't loud and boisterous, quiet and reflective, action driven, or sedentary. It's all of those, as the Spirit moves and as we respond. The Bible gives us countless examples of people using the entirety of who they are to reach for God.

They raise their hands. "*I will praise you as long as I live, and in your name I will lift up my hands*" (Psalm 63:4 NIV).

They bow their knees. "*Come, let us bow down in worship, let us kneel before the LORD our Maker*" (Psalm 95:6 NIV).

They dance for joy. "*Let them praise His name with dancing and make music to him with timbrel and harp*" (Psalm 149:3 NIV).

Honestly, I feel like I've only begun to explore the benefits of incorporating my body into my prayers, but the new habits I'm forming as I learn to worship God with my body are bearing fruit. I may not always have ready words in prayer. My soul may be stressed. My spirit troubled. But guess what I've discovered? Even in those moments, I can move my body. I can kneel. I can raise my hands in worship of the God I know and the faith in my heart, even if (especially if) doubts are assailing me. Many times, I've walked toward the lake behind my house, empty, upset, and wounded but bent on sitting on the dock and taking my heart to

God. And I've seen the spirit that lives in this body stirred out of its lethargy time and again, all because I moved my God-given body toward the One who formed it.

USE THE BODY YOU HAVE TO REACH FOR THE GOD YOU LOVE.

The experience reminds me of a quote from *The Screwtape Letters* by C. S. Lewis. The demonic Screwtape is counseling his twisted student, Wormwood, when he offers this reminder about the humans his protégé is tasked with deceiving:

> At the very least, they can be persuaded that the bodily position makes no difference to their prayers; for they constantly forget, what you must always remember, that they are animals and that whatever their bodies do affects their souls.[8]

So much truth there. We are both verbal and nonverbal people. Experts disagree on how much of our communication is nonverbal, but it's clear that our body language is undeniably loud. We wave to greet each other. We jump in joy. Fans high-five when their team wins and lovers take a knee to pledge their love. We lean forward to make a point during conversation; we lean back to register our hesitation. There are entire fields of study devoted to our body language. So why would we try to pray with only words without using the language of the body we use in the rest of our lives?

I want to encourage you to step out of your comfort zone and use the body God gave you to love Him with all of your strength. That could be kneeling. It could be dancing. It could be lifting your hands in worship. Or if you're a nondenominational Jesus lover who was raised Baptist, it could mean you begin making the sign

8. C. S. Lewis, *The Screwtape Letters* (New York: Macmillan Co., 1943), 25.

of the cross over your body. Yes, there's a story here. Feel free to add this confession to all the other ones I've made in this book.

Growing up, I saw Catholic friends crossing themselves and I thought it was just a superstitious gesture. And at times, that might be all it is, but don't we all go through the motions and do things out of habit without engaging our hearts? I have no doubt the practice can be rote and religious, but it can also be spontaneous and moving.

Signing oneself with the cross dates to the earliest days of Christianity. At its inception, the cross was traced on the forehead and only later were the chest and shoulders included. It began as a sign of ongoing devotion and commitment. It's a real-time profession of faith and an acknowledgement that our bodies are the temples of God, which is how many practice it today, myself included. After learning all of this history, I felt moved to begin making the sign of the cross over my own body, as a way of yielding to God in the moment. I started by closing my morning prayers with it, but crossing myself has since become a sweet part of my days, and my prayer life is the stronger for it.

Hugs,
Shellie

Pray with Me

Dear Lord, we're prone to trying to disassociate ourselves from our bodies when we pray. Forgive us. When You made us, You called Your creation good. We want to worship You with our bodies as well as our minds and our spirits. Teach us how to do this. Help us learn to move to Your honor and Your glory. We pray in the sweet name of Your Son and our Savior, Jesus the Lord. Amen.

Practice with Me

For my non-Catholic readers, the sign of the cross is made by touching your forehead with your fingers as you say "Father," to your chest as you say "Son," and then to your right shoulder and left shoulder as you say "Holy Spirit." Try it, with sincerity and intentionality, and combine it with your own prayer words. I like to follow it with whatever is applicable at the moment. Sometimes that means I sign myself and after I say, "Father, Son, and Holy Spirit," I add, "I commit myself to You." Other times I might finish with, "Strengthen me." And sometimes ... ah, sometimes, I simply take a huge heavenly breath and end on this soul-soothing note, "I am Yours." What prayer might you use with the sign of the cross?

A FEW CLOSING THOUGHTS

This has been one of the more difficult books I've written to date. I was probably halfway through this work when I began telling an author friend of my writer angst. In trying to articulate my feelings, I finally came to understand why this one was testing me so sorely—which, ironically, speaks to one more reason we should pray. Sometimes, we have no idea what's in our hearts until we pour them out to the Lord.

Ironically, it has been my commitment to being as open as possible about my ongoing prayer journey that has made this work so challenging. It can be encouraging to learn alongside someone who freely admits to being both pupil and instructor, so I've aimed to do as much of that as possible in these pages. I just hope I've done it without causing you to question your decision to accept prayer habits from someone who hasn't made it further down the road. As it stands, I can only pray (no pun intended) that my zeal for God's presence has been every bit as obvious and you've found it equally sincere.

Considering the challenge this book has been from start to finish, no one could be more surprised than I am to find I'm ambivalent about wrapping it up! I would have thought I'd be throwing a party when this day arrived. Instead, I feel more like a mother watching her child take that next step that's going to lead them away from her. Whether they're graduating preschool, high school, or college, moving away to take their first job, or about to marry their true loves, we always feel like there are things we should have said. Did we tell them everything? What did we forget and what will they remember? It's not like I don't realize there are countless other books on prayer you can pick up once you put this one down, but my personal opportunity to help you is winding down with these last words. So I sit here, wondering what else I could have said or should have said.

I'm thinking of the things that help me pray that didn't find their way into one of these chapters, like my fondness for having my Bible open on my lap. That's a fairly new practice, but I'm finding I love feeling its holy weight as I pray. And I could've told you about the joy I find in taking secular songs and rewriting them with lyrics that praise Jesus and how this often positions my heart in prayer. Jesus is seriously the only one who enjoys my singing voice, but He and I have a grand ol' time at these off-key concerts. Oh, and there's the habit I've developed while driving, the one where I take all the signs and buildings around me and fill the trip with a string of one-line prayers. I shared this idea with my bestie years ago, and we've often embraced it for miles on road trips. If we see a bank, we rejoice in Jesus, our strong tower and heavenly defense. A grocery store leads us to celebrate His provision. If you can believe it, we've even been known to turn vape outlets into prayer moments. Not even joking. It sounds like, "Lord, Your Word tells us we're mere vapors. Teach us to number our days." (Perhaps you can see why I didn't give that one its own chapter.)

But seriously, there's something else pressing on me right now. It was hovering just out of sight when I began these closing thoughts. I couldn't quite put my finger on what was weighing on me. But the realization has since crystallized and with it has come an urgency to address a more serious issue before our time is over. I want to take a minute to talk about how to keep praying when what you're praying for isn't changing and you've prayed until you don't think you have the words or the will to say one more prayer. We've all been there. Some of us are there right now.

First, I get it. The longer we pray about the same thing, without it being resolved, the more likely we are to become discouraged and quit going to God with it. Or—and this is equally sad if not more so—we resort to phoning our prayers in with hearts that are growing increasingly cold and distant. When we know God can act and He isn't, we can begin doubting He ever will, and if we allow that thought to take root, a serious rift can form between us and our Father. Books upon books have been written by serious Bible scholars expounding on why bad things keep happening to good people, and why some prayers are answered and others aren't. I won't be adding my thoughts to theirs. Instead, I want to speak to you about how to find the will to keep pressing in and why you'll be glad if you do.

Spoiler? Holy Spirit is the answer to both of those questions.

None of us have what it takes in ourselves to stay in the fight and keep praying over the long haul when we can't see how our prayers are changing anything. The secret is to own this weakness! Own it and learn to live running to the well that never runs dry. If we ask, Holy Spirit will help us keep praying and keep believing. And the longer we linger with God, the more we position ourselves to experience Him in ways we didn't expect and didn't know we needed.

> *Call to Me, and I will answer you, and show you great and mighty things, which you do not know.* (Jeremiah 33:3 NKJV)

That verse is mind-bending in the best way. Almighty God promises not only to answer us but to tell us what we don't know. I love to tell Him that leaves a wide-open field for Him to tell me most anything! It's in the asking, seeking, and knocking (see Matthew 7:7–8) that we find this fresh perspective, and it can help us confront aspects of a hard situation we haven't considered and give us new ways to pray. And when we stay there, soaking in His presence, our hope is renewed and our faith grows stronger in the waiting. Praise Him, Holy Spirit is the *how* to keep praying. Don't try to pray without asking for His help and don't try to keep praying without depending on Him!

Again, I can't tell you why our sovereign God answers some prayers with a *yes*, some with a *no*, and some with what seems like painful silence. I can, however, tell you about one prayer that never gets a *no* from heaven. The believer's sincere cry for fresh resources from Holy Spirit meets an eternal *yes* in Christ Jesus. And there's our *why*. Why will we be glad we continued to pray? Because our spirits hunger to experience the reality of God, and He affirms His presence to those who live seeking Him. Nothing life offers is sweeter. Holy Spirit keeps our hearts from growing cold as we learn how to wait on Him.

NOTHING LIFE OFFERS IS SWEETER THAN EXPERIENCING THE REALITY OF GOD.

One last story...

These days, my dog-loving heart belongs to a hundred-pound white Labrador Retriever named Hank, but Hank had a predecessor named Dixie Belle who lives in our family's memories and now resides forever in her favorite resting spot beside our driveway. Dixie Belle was a brown Lab with a love for chasing a tennis ball that topped anything we had ever seen. Dixie wasn't simply *fond* of playing fetch; she had a neurotic obsession with *retrieving* that meant the human tossing the ball to her had to know when to say when—because Dixie Belle didn't have it in her to quit. From the moment we walked outdoors, Dixie had one goal: get someone to toss her ball and keep tossing it!

Early one morning, I took a seat under the big old oak tree in our backyard. I had my Bible in one hand and my coffee in the other. Tears were streaming down my face as I sat down to pray about something I'd already prayed about a thousand times before. All I could think at the time was *why*. Why wasn't the Lord intervening? Why wasn't He changing the situation?

As usual, Dixie found me immediately and determined it was time to play. She dropped her tennis ball in front of me and waited, her dark brown eyes eager. When I didn't comply, she repeated her request a good dozen times or more. Pick up ball, drop it, pick up ball, drop it, tail wagging with expectation. Perhaps it was my heartsickness driving it, but I decided Dixie needed a lesson in patience and there was no better time for it.

"No, Dixie. Not right now. I'm praying."

And I was, or at least I was trying to, but God and I both knew my thoughts were more accusation than adoration.

Dixie picked up her ball and dropped it at my feet, again.

"Lord," I complained … I mean prayed. "You can change this. Why won't you?"

Dixie picked up her yellow ball and dropped it directly on my foot. "No, Dixie." Over the next few minutes, the scene repeated itself countless times.

Dixie whined at me.

I whined at the Father.

Dixie recovered her ball and dropped in on my feet, again. "I love you, Dixie," I thought to myself, "but you need to learn to wait on me." Meanwhile, I searched for prayer words and impatiently tossed them toward the heavens, again.

I'm sure you're beginning to see what took me much longer to realize. I do remember at some point taking Dixie's face in my hands and saying, "I love you, girl. But I'm trying to do something here you just can't understand, and I need you to trust me."

And that was it—the moment I realized Father God was saying the same thing to me. My ears didn't hear His words, but my heart felt them and I knew we weren't talking about a tennis ball any longer, but the ongoing situation that was trying my soul. "I love you, Shellie, but I'm doing something here you just can't understand. Will you trust Me?"

I sensed the Lord waiting, as if I was being given time to answer honestly. I didn't need it. There was only one answer because I knew the Father's eyes were on me and His ears were open to my cries. That knowledge helped me rest in His love. *Yes, Lord. I'll trust You.*

Trouble can come to us from so many directions. Some of the troubles we encounter in this life are the fruit of our own sin. Sometimes, our troubles are thrust upon us by the choices other people make. Still others are merely the result of living in a fallen world that continues to rebel against and resist its Maker. But our Savior God promises us in Romans 8:28 that, "*God causes all things to work together for good to those who love God, to those who are called according to His purpose.*" All things. God takes the good and the bad and works them all together into His will and purpose for our lives and His kingdom, and He does this weaving together for those who love Him regardless of where the trouble originated. I can't explain it, but I've experienced it.

I didn't mean to leave you hanging with that Dixie story. I sense your questions. Was God just waiting on me to surrender? Did the situation get fixed asap once I yielded to His timing? And was that the last time I've ever struggled with unanswered prayers? No, no, and no. But I continue to seek Him through it all because tasting the presence of God ruins you for anything less than more of Him.

By the way, Dixie remained obsessed with her tennis ball for the rest of her precious canine years, and I doubt she ever understood why I was quick to throw it on some days and not others. Over time, however, she became more and more satisfied to just be with me until my *amen* signaled it was time for action.

For some time now, I've been telling the Lord I want my life to be a prayer. As I taste more and more of His friendship, as I discover new expressions of adoration, like breathing my prayers and using body language to reach toward Him, my desire for His company continues to grow. This is what I want for you. Long after you close this book, when you can't even remember my name, I hope you'll be calling on His. He is more than enough, and He is worthy.

My prayer is that you'll stay after Jesus until He become home to you. That even when your thoughts leave to attend to things of this world, they'll hurry back to Him just as quickly. It is possible for Him to be home, to know life where we don't resort to Him but live from Him. I can't say I've mastered it, but I can testify that when I do, I want to learn such living all the more.

Hugs,
Shellie

"THROUGH THE DOOR"

There's a Door to God —
a solid way
to enjoy His Presence —
every day.

It's not a formula,
distant and cold —
I tell of a Savior…
the Shepherd of old.

Once I paced the Open Door —
so conscious of my need for more.
Always working — to abide,
… seldom making it inside.

Then I discovered grace galore
is owning my need
right at the Door!
No more trying to pray just right —
I run through that Door
with all my might.

With empty hands...
and muddy feet...
I race headlong
to Mercy's seat.

There Jesus washes
and tends my soul.
He comforts, guides...
and makes me whole.

Sweet the well that ever flows,
All my need — the Savior knows.
May everything I do and say,
Point others to this Blessed Way.

Through the Door
where mercy meets...
with open arms
and nail-scarred feet.

ABOUT THE AUTHOR

Shellie Rushing Tomlinson is an award-winning, multi-published author, speaker, and farmer's wife known for saying, "Life can be hard when it's good, but it's always better when you're laughing." Shellie excels at using humor and storytelling to unpack biblical truth aimed at helping others discover the lives Jesus died to give them.

Jeff Foxworthy endorsed her award-winning humor books *Suck Your Stomach In and Put Some Color On* and *Sue Ellen's Girl Ain't Fat, She Just Weighs Heavy!* Shellie's Christian nonfiction works include *Seizing the Good Life* and *Heart Wide Open*.

After more than a decade in radio, Shellie now hosts *The Story Table* podcast and cohosts the popular *Rocking It Grand* podcast with her friend, Chrys Howard, on the Christian Parenting network.

Shellie and her husband, Phil, live and farm in Lake Providence, Louisiana. They have two grown children and six grandchildren.

Connect with Shellie:

shelliet.com

writeshellie@gmail.com

Website

Facebook

Instagram